The Right Instrument for your Child

Atarah Ben-Tovim was a teenage prodigy on the flute, playing concertos with professional symphony orchestras from the age of fifteen. Her husband, author Douglas Boyd, was a BBC television producer and a musical drop-out. Together they created Atarah's Band, a unique live music show for children which earned them the MBE in 1980. Atarah's pioneering work in matching children with instruments was recognized in 1991 by the award of an honorary Doctorate of Music.

The Right Instrument for your Child

ATARAH BEN-TOVIM
and DOUGLAS BOYD

Weidenfeld & Nicolson
LONDON

First published in Great Britain in 1985
by Victor Gollancz Ltd

This edition published in 2005
by Weidenfeld & Nicolson

1 3 5 7 9 10 8 6 4 2

A CIP catalogue record for this book
is available from the British Library.

ISBN 0 297 85065 2

Typeset at The Spartan Press Ltd,
Lymington, Hants

Printed in Great Britain by
Clays Ltd, St Ives plc

Weidenfeld & Nicolson
The Orion Publishing Group Ltd
Orion House
5 Upper Saint Martin's Lane
London WC2H 9EA

www.orionbooks.co.uk

Contents

Foreword to the Fourth Edition

For the past thirty years I have been counselling parents and teachers on how to select the best instrument for individual children to learn.

Twenty years ago Livia Gollancz – herself a successful musician – asked me to write the first edition of *The Right Instrument for your Child*. In the intervening years, many thousands of parents and teachers have successfully used the step-by-step system in this book to give their children the best possible start on the path to making music. In so doing they have found it possible to invert the normal failure rate: their letters testify that whereas nine out of ten children on randomly allocated instruments drop out, nine out of ten succeed on a properly chosen instrument!

Failure to learn an instrument impoverishes a whole lifetime by frustrating the desire to make music which is latent within us all. So it is not an exaggeration to say that the correct choice of instrument is the key to unlocking your child's musical potential.

Atarah Ben-Tovim, MBE, Hon.DMus, ARAM, LRAM, ARCM

Introduction

Why should any child learn a musical instrument today?

With increasing pressure on children to achieve high academic results, some parents question whether it is worth spending time, money and energy on the lengthy process of learning an instrument. The answer is that it has never been so worthwhile. Apart from the joy of being able to make music, there are more reasons to learn an instrument than ever before.

Often it improves a child's classroom performance; educationists themselves accuse in-school education of being too verbal and left-hemisphere centred, whereas making music is a non-verbal activity which nourishes the right hemisphere of the brain and makes for a more balanced person, better able to achieve his or her academic potential.

Gradual mastery of the instrument builds self-confidence, and making music, either alone or in peer groups, is a releasing therapy for any adolescent. As college and university tutors know, students are less likely to drop out if they have the self-motivation and self-discipline which is naturally acquired in learning an instrument.

The rewards in adult life are many. Mastery of an instrument may lead to a job as an orchestral or freelance musician.

More will find work as in-school or private music teachers and music therapists. If these are obvious career opportunities, there is also a long list of other professions open to musically educated job-seekers.

Taking music exams, participating in competitions and playing in a school band or youth orchestra are all excellent preparation for making the best impression at job interviews and selection boards. And a Grade 5 or Grade 8 certificate enhances any c.v. or job application.

In an age of increasing leisure, sometimes unsought, it is impossible to over-estimate the lifelong joy of being able to make music and to understand it on a level that no non-player ever reaches. 'If only I had learnt to play an instrument,' is surely one of the saddest phrases ever uttered in later life.

The Mozart Effect

There is much serious evidence that playing high-frequency classical music to babies and young children enhances their intellectual development. If simply hearing the music can work in this way, how much more effective is learning to play this music – a physical and mental process which positively involves the body as well as the conscious and subconscious intelligence. From a very early stage of learning, playing parts written in the upper register or high and middle frequencies – as all beginner music is – imprints the child's developing brain with non-verbal mental activity conceived by highly intelligent composers, many of whom are recognized geniuses.

One could fill a serious specialist tome with examples, but a single anecdote may make the point. Many years ago, after a recital in a famous public school, the music master informed me that the headmaster insisted on every pupil learning an instrument to intermediate level. Astounded to learn that this headmaster was tone-deaf, I asked why he thought music so important for his charges. The reply was that half a century's experience of teaching had convinced him that learning an instrument produced what he called 'better people'. Since he could not appreciate the music at the school concerts, he was unaffected by any artistic pretensions and was judging only academic results.

For all these reasons, the selection of an instrument is a decision-making process that every parent will want to get right.

Choosing an Instrument

There are two ways of choosing an instrument. In the traditional hit-or-miss approach the child starts piano lessons because there is a teacher nearby or is given a violin that happens to be available. Or maybe he or she has said, 'I'd like to play the . . .'

Statistically such a child has one chance in ten of succeeding. For the other 90 per cent, after a few months, the problems of learning a badly chosen instrument result in a loss of interest; this has nothing to do with intelligence or 'musicality'. Lessons continue because of pressure from the adults involved and a battle of wills develops between child and parents/teachers who use bullying, bribery or cajolery to ensure minimal practice and attendance at weekly lessons.

The child is left with only one way of demonstrating his or her individuality: by skimping practice and skipping lessons whenever there is an excuse. Anyone can see that this is a waste of the child's time – and probably the parents' money as well. What is not so obvious is that the child feels a lifelong sense of failure, has learnt that he or she is 'no good at music', and feels cheated.

The second way of choosing an instrument is the systematic one, in which the parent deals with each aspect of the choice separately and in logical order. The Ben-Tovim/Boyd System includes all the information necessary but leaves the parent in complete charge of the decisions.

The Ben-Tovim/Boyd Instrument Matching System

This book is the result of a unique programme of research which involved several thousand parents and children. Every piece of advice has been tried and tested in consultation with teachers, musicians, doctors, dentists, psychologists, youth workers and other specialists.

The authors stand on both sides of the musical divide: an ex-prodigy and an ex-drop-out. The prodigy was already playing concertos with professional symphony orchestras on television in her early teens; the drop-out gave up the piano after three years of humiliation and frustration. Because our own childhood experiences spanned the gamut of public success and private failure, we were interested to know whether children can really be divided into 'musical' and 'unmusical' as some people believe.

To avoid being influenced or biased by anyone or any organization, we set up the Ben-Tovim Music Research Centre in the Pennine hills north of Manchester. At the Centre and on our travels in Britain and abroad, we interviewed children from a wide range of educational and social backgrounds who were learning instruments, together with a control group who had given up on music.

In all our research we found no evidence that the drop-outs were less musical than their co-evals playing in school bands, county youth orchestras and so on. Other independent surveys have found that advanced music students are no more musical than fellow students reading geography or social sciences. Why then do some drop out and some go on to succeed?

In our survey we found that most children have a musical capability far beyond what is necessary to learn to play the right instrument. There was overwhelming evidence that the drop-outs had been wrongly advised or encouraged by adults to begin learning instruments on which they were individually bound to fail from the start. Choosing the wrong instrument was the most common factor in musical failure – not lack of musicality or musical potential.

Playing an instrument is a physical activity which also involves intelligence and emotions. No child is a carbon copy of another, so the first stage in this system is for the parent to assess the child in terms which make selection of the right instrument a logical process.

The second stage is a Three-Way Examination of each instrument which reveals its suitability/unsuitability for the child. This automatically produces a Short List. No prior musical knowledge is required.

The third stage is to eliminate the less suitable instruments from the Short List and arrive at the Right One!

The Ben-Tovim/Boyd Instrument Matching System

STAGE ONE: ASSESSING YOUR CHILD

Musicality Test

Readiness Test

Assessing your Child

Physique
Mentality
Personality

Three-Way Profile

STAGE TWO: EVALUATING THE INSTRUMENTS

Sorting out the Instruments

Three-Way Examination of the Instruments

Physical Suitability
Mental Suitability
Personality Suitability

Suitability Summaries

Short List

The Right Instrument

Stage One

Assessing your Child

The level of musicality necessary to learn a systematically chosen instrument is so universal that it can be checked by this simple test.

Musicality Test

Circle round the appropriate answer.

PART A: ABILITIES

Can the child:
- recognize the theme music of favourite TV shows? YES / NO
- join in with 'pop' at the right time when you sing 'Pop Goes The Weasel'? YES / NO
- tell which is the high note when you sing HEE-HAW with HEE high and HAW low? YES / NO
- clap back to you a simple rhythm you tap out on the table? (Use the first two lines of 'Baa Baa Black Sheep'.) YES / NO
- identify correctly, with eyes closed, the sounds of you tapping

(a) a glass and (b) a small saucepan? YES / NO
(Rehearse this with eyes open first.)

- sing or whistle accurately a familiar TV theme or song, when asked to do so? YES / NO
- complete the melody if you sing the first half of a known tune? (E.g. Parent: Baa baa black sheep, have you any wool? Child: Yes sir, yes sir, three bags full.) YES / NO
- name three or more musical instruments? YES / NO
- name one, or more than one, instrumental musician? YES / NO

PART B: ACTIVITIES

Does the child:
- enjoy listening to music? YES / NO
- respond physically to music? YES / NO
- have some favourite music on record or cassette which he/she plays frequently? YES / NO
- repeatedly express a desire to play a certain instrument? (This will not necessarily be the right one.) YES / NO

If you have circled YES fewer than eight times, this does not necessarily mean that your child is unmusical. Most likely, he or she is too young – or too much occupied with school or other pressures – to begin developing musically.

In that case, do the Test again in a few months' time. Meanwhile, try to make a richer musical environment for the child. Choose a wide range of music for him or her to listen to, watch musical programmes on television together, discuss favourite tunes or which sounds are liked or disliked and why. If possible, take the child to some live events where musicians can be seen and heard – from circuses to brass bands to school concerts.

If you have circled YES eight or more times, your child is musical enough to play an instrument. Whether or not this potential is realized, depends on two things, both of them in your control:

- choosing the right instrument, i.e. one with no physical, mental or emotional drawbacks for your child; and
- starting to learn at the right time.

Is your child ready to start learning an instrument?

Every major stage of a child's development happens in its own good time. Some children naturally walk or talk much earlier than others and nobody finds this strange. Yet when it comes to music, some teachers will tell you that violin lessons should begin by the age of three or four; in other countries educational authorities recommend starting as late as thirteen or fourteen (which is when many musicians first take up their professional instruments). It can be very confusing.

Yet timing the start of learning to play is vital because in all our thousands of interviews, the second most common factor in musical failure was starting at the wrong time – too early.

The right moment for your child is not simply a question of age, but a coincidence of physical, mental and emotional development. It occurs later than one might think and falls most often between the ages of seven and eleven.

Many parents throw up their hands in horror when they hear this. 'Our six-year-old says every day, "I want to play the violin/piano/flute." So we're going to buy an instrument and start lessons – even if he is a bit young.'

It is true that a six-year-old who goes on and on about

wanting to play a musical instrument is experiencing the promptings of his developing instinct to make music, but he is not yet ready to do much about it. The instinct will naturally ebb and return more strongly in a year or two. What he actually feels is too diffuse for a small child to put into words, so he invents a specific achievement fantasy and tells his parents, 'I want to be a trumpeter.'

Although this may sound to an adult ear like a mature decision to start all the hard work of learning an instrument, it should be treated more on the lines of: 'I want to be a racing driver/nurse/astronaut.'

'But what about even younger children who start learning and seem to make progress?' parents ask. In almost every case, those children are being 'pushed' by a musically educated or musically frustrated parent who attends the weekly lessons and supervises daily practice sessions in detail. The parent provides the motivation to begin and to continue, and tells the child what to do all the time. Suzuki classes are an example. Unless you are that kind of parent and intend to commit a regular part of every day for several years to this shared musical education, the extra risks of starting early are not justified.

Some parents wonder whether children who start instrumental lessons early will have some advantage over those who begin later. The answer is: very little, if any. Remember that what takes a five-year-old three years to master can be achieved by an eight-year-old in a few months! So use the Readiness Test. Like the Musicality Test, it looks simple – but it works.

Readiness Test

Can the child:

- already read fluently? YES / NO
- write without problems? YES / NO
- do simple addition, multiplication, subtraction and division? YES / NO
- handle the social pressures of school? YES / NO

Has the child:

- attended full-time school for at least two and a half years? YES / NO
- carried on any hobby or belonged to an out-of-school activity or interest group for three months or more? YES / NO
- know the difference between work and play? YES / NO
- have the spare mental energy (after schoolwork is done) to begin a demanding new activity? YES / NO

YES to every question means a child who is ready to begin the great adventure of learning an instrument.

A single NO indicates a child who is not yet ready, no matter how good school reports may be.

If in doubt, it is always better to wait.

This does not mean wasting time because there is an interim musical adventure which is great fun for child and parent. You can teach your child basic recorder technique.

Before you say or think, 'I can't do that,' the answer is that you can. If children of six or eight are capable of learning to play simple tunes on the recorder, it stands to reason that any adult can teach him- or herself, in order to teach the child.

Buy a couple of descant recorders and a tutor book. Teach

yourself one lesson ahead of the child, and off you go! So long as the whole thing is treated as fun, you can do nothing but good. There is no need to push on to the next lesson in a hurry. Some children enjoy playing the same tune for months. 'Go and Tell Aunt Nancy' played for the thousandth time may drive you mad, but if that is the natural level of your child's *present* musical ambition, let it be.

If interest wanes, it is probably because the child has come into a period of stress at school. Wait until he or she has some more energy to spare and then re-start the recorder sessions. In the meantime, you may have forgotten some of what was learnt but the child will not have done.

And don't forget the human voice! Sing with and to your child. Encourage him or her to sing to you and with you. If you are insecure about your own voice (perhaps because you were told not to sing in school music lessons or daily assembly) buy some singalong tapes and enjoy listening together as well.

At this stage, so long as it's fun, it's good.

The Three-Way Profile

If a child is both musical enough to learn and ready to begin, the next step is to draw up his or her Three-Way Profile against which to assess the instruments one by one in Stage Two.

Do not be tempted to omit the Profile. The traps from which it saves you include:

- selecting a self-contained instrument like piano or guitar for a sociable child, *however right that may seem for his or her brain;*

- choosing an instrument that satisfies emotional needs but whose music is too difficult or *too easy*;
- deciding on an instrument that suits mentality and temperament *yet is physically uncomfortable*.

If the last point seems strange, remember the pleasure principle! In the early stages, the physical enjoyment of playing a well-chosen instrument is the most important reason why the child wants to practise each day.

The parts of the body and aspects of mentality and personality that govern the choice of instrument are each listed in the three assessment charts below.

The first one is the easiest chart to use, inasmuch as every parent knows whether the child is overweight, has long arms, lacks some second teeth, etc.

The other two charts will probably take longer. School reports may be helpful but equally important are the child's attitudes and behaviour in the home and with friends, as well as his or her hobbies and leisure interests.

To succeed on the right instrument, a child does not have to be good at schoolwork. Most schools and teachers denigrate those characteristics which make life in the classroom difficult, so that 'impatient', 'slow-learning' and 'can't concentrate' are criticized as defects when they are really no more than indicators of how the child reacts to the classroom environment. Some of the characteristics which teachers dislike most can actually lead to success in learning an instrument. And many children who are under-valued at school make excellent progress on an instrument – perhaps partly because they have been denied achievement in the classroom. Happily, this in turn helps them cope with the problems they formerly had at school.

To make your child's Three-Way Profile, circle the words

which apply to him or her on the charts. There are no right or wrong answers, so there is no point in cheating in order to create a more favourable picture of the child. This is an impulse entirely natural to a caring parent, but just for once, you must resist it!

Circle round the words that apply to your child

EYESIGHT
excellent
normal
astigmatic
wears spectacles

HEARING
acute
normal
below normal

LIPS
thin
average
thick

MOUTH CONTROL
can whistle
can't whistle

FRONT TEETH
protruding
normal
receding

FRONT TEETH
large
average
small

FRONT TEETH
even and regular
irregular

DENTAL DEVELOPMENT
first teeth
second teeth coming through
second teeth firm in gums

LUNGS/BREATHING
asthmatic/bronchitic
average
strong

REACH OF ARMS
short
average for height
long

HAND-SPAN
can span an octave on piano
can't span an octave*

FINGERS
short
average
long

* 7½ inches or 19 centimetres

LITTLE FINGER
short
average
long

BREADTH OF FINGER PADS
narrow
average
broad

DEXTERITY
left-handed
right-handed

PHYSICAL CO-ORDINATION
clumsy
normal
well co-ordinated

PHYSICAL ENERGY
energetic
average
sedentary

PHYSICAL ENERGY
enjoys sports
not sporting
lacks energy

GENERAL HEALTH
delicate
normal
robust

GENERAL PHYSIQUE
tall
average for age
short

GENERAL PHYSIQUE
overweight
average
thin

PHYSICAL FEELING
likes putting things in mouth
does not like it

PHYSICAL FEELING
likes vibration against lips*
does not like it

Such as a kazoo, or comb and tissue paper

ASSESSING YOUR CHILD ➤ MENTALITY

Circle round the words that apply to your child.

MENTAL TYPE
logical/mathematical
intuitive/artistic

SPEED OF LEARNING
quick
average
slow

MEMORY
good
average
finds memorizing difficult

READING
reads habitually, for pleasure
can read fluently
not fluent

WRITING
fluent
not fluent

MATHEMATICS
likes the subject
can do it
has problems

MENTAL ARITHMETIC
finds it easy

average
finds it hard

CONCENTRATION
daydreams often
average
concentrates well

PERSISTENCE
needs quick results
prepared to 'plod along'

ATTITUDE TO SCHOOLWORK
has problems
no problems at school

SCHOOL ACHIEVEMENT
near top of class
average
below average

APPLICATION
lazy
works if pushed
conscientious

SPARE MENTAL ENERGY
AFTER SCHOOL
plenty
some
none

*The following chart can be difficult to use because your child's person-
ality interacts with your own in normal family life. Two adult brains may
be better than one, to obtain objectivity.*

ASSESSING YOUR CHILD ➤ PERSONALITY

Which of these alternatives describes your child? Circle them.

generous	OR	acquisitive
a few special friends	OR	many friends
calm	OR	lively
bright, quick-witted	OR	dreamy, forgetful
quiet	OR	boisterous
some hobbies	OR	no leisure interests
solitary	OR	sociable, gregarious
prefers physical activity	OR	prefers mental activities
outgoing	OR	shy
enjoys relating to adults	OR	doesn't enjoy relating to adults
likes parents to be involved	OR	likes to be independent of family
easygoing	OR	ambitious
determined	OR	gives up easily
self-centred	OR	sensitive to others
academic	OR	creative
patient	OR	impatient
attention-seeking	OR	prefers not to be noticed
dominant, bossy	OR	responsive, likes others to lead
peaceable	OR	aggressive
soft, gentle	OR	hard, tough
moody	OR	even-tempered
casual	OR	intense
serious	OR	fun-seeking
self-disciplined	OR	fidgety
responsible	OR	doesn't like responsibility
good-natured	OR	has fits of temper
'difficult'	OR	well-balanced
stubborn	OR	easily led
good at modelling or needlework	OR	'bad with hands'

You will be surprised how easy your child's Three-Way Profile makes the selection or rejection of each instrument in Stage Two.

To guide your decisions, we have set out hundreds of facts about the instruments. Many are unknown even to professional teachers and musicians because musical education tends to produce specialists who know a lot about one instrument or one family of instruments and very little about the others. Rarely will a flute-player, for example, know much about the brass; nor will a percussionist be able to tell you much about the strings.

It is for this reason that parents often receive wrong or misleading advice from musicians and teachers. Even if they were to approach an orchestral conductor – who does have a reasonably comprehensive knowledge of many instruments – there is no guarantee that even he will know much about non-orchestral instruments. Nor is he able to comment on the appropriateness of individual instruments for your child.

You are the expert on your child. By the time you have worked through Stage Two, you will know everything you need to know about the instruments.

Stage Two

Evaluating the Instruments

Sorting out the Instruments

Any reasonably large music shop offers you today a range of instruments at prices suitable for children to learn on – a range which is larger than ever before. This is because modern methods of instrument manufacture have actually reduced the real cost of most student instruments.

Of course, that is a good thing, but many parents find the sheer extent of the range of instruments disturbing. They are tempted to seek refuge in the much smaller range of instruments which are familiar: piano, violin, guitar and maybe, flute.

If you are one of these parents who would feel at a disadvantage on walking into a music shop and being confronted by shelves and showcases full of instruments, use our simple system to sort them all out.

The instruments are like a pack of cards. In the same way that it can be difficult to distinguish one instrument from another when they are all jumbled together in a shop, so it is hard to check that all the cards are there – and none missing – if the pack has been scattered at random across the table.

What do you do? You separate the cards into their four suits, and then make sure you have all the cards in each suit. If there are some jokers or other odd cards, you deal with them last.

That system works just as well for sorting out the instruments. There are four suits, or main groups, of instruments:

- the Woodwind
- the Brass
- the Stringed Instruments
- the Percussion.

The 'jokers' are:

- the Self-Contained Instruments
- the Self-Taught Instruments.

Three-Way Examination of the Instruments

All the instruments have one thing in common: they were designed, or evolved, as machines to be operated by the body of a fully grown man. No instrument was designed to be operated by the body of a six-year-old, or even an eleven-year-old child.

Some instruments are highly developed machines – such as the piano which does most of the physical work for the player. Only three instruments are made in small sizes: the violin, guitar and cello. (For technical reasons, other instruments would not function properly if their sizes were reduced.) Yet, size and physical ease of operation do not make any instrument automatically suitable for children. In fact, the piano, violin and guitar are among the most difficult instruments to learn – and have the highest failure rates.

It is a coincidence if a child can physically manage an instrument designed for an adult to play. Some instruments are too heavy, or too large, or require too much energy for a child. True, some children may play them, but your child would be uncomfortable, or even stressed, trying to play these instruments. Why should any child – or adult – go on doing something which is uncomfortable or stressful? Physical discomfort is a great reason for giving up an instrument.

So, first and foremost, the right instrument is one which is physically comfortable for the child to hold and play – because he or she happens to have the developed physical characteristics which are important for playing that instrument.

This physical matching is not just a question of the child fulfilling the requirements of the instrument. In return, the child must get certain physical rewards.

Playing any instrument has a particular sensation, because of the way in which the player's body is used in the process of playing. We call this 'physical feed-back'. Some children like the feed-back, or sensation, of playing the violin; others are left cold by it. Some children like the feeling of an oboe or clarinet reed vibrating in the mouth; others hate it.

Physical Suitability is a compound: the child fulfils the requirements of the instrument without stress or discomfort; in return, the child gets the reward of a physical feed-back which he or she finds pleasurable. Physical pleasure from playing the instrument is the most powerful reason of all why a child should carry on learning.

The right instrument gives the child physical pleasure, without stress or discomfort.

You can see at a glance that the physical requirements of playing, say, the flute and the double bass are very different. Whilst you cannot see the difference in mental requirements of the various instruments, they are equally important.

Playing a single-note instrument, such as cornet or flute, requires far less mental energy than a chordal instrument such as guitar or piano. Yet, a mechanically simple old instrument such as the violin demands vastly more mental energy than the recently invented saxophone.

Some children have a brain which does one thing at a time. Other children, who may be good at mental arithmetic or chess, find pleasure in complexity – dealing with several things apparently at the same moment. One-thing-at-a-timers find their pleasure on single-note instruments, while those who are top of the class at mental arithmetic find the complexity of the chordal instruments a satisfying, but never demoralizing, challenge.

The right instrument gives the child no mental stress, but the continuing stimulation of doing something which his or her brain finds natural.

The third way in which an instrument must suit the child involves the emotions, or personality, of the player. This may sound a little diffuse, but the information about each instrument is set out so that this aspect is no more difficult to deal with than the other two.

Certain instruments suit certain kinds of children. Hyper-active children are a nightmare for a violin teacher, but a dream for percussionists. The very sound made by an instrument appeals more to certain children than to others. A gentle, wistful child drawn to the sound of the viola would be unhappy on the oboe and probably could not play the trumpet without pain.

Some instruments are solitary. A sociable, outgoing child who is learning classical guitar or piano is bound to be frustrated and unhappy because he will have no chance of playing with others for many years to come. Conversely, a truly solitary child will be miserable on a brass instrument, which is used for making music only in bands or orchestras.

The right instrument satisfies and develops the emotional side of the child's nature and does not frustrate it.

The Three-Way Profile of your child makes it easy and uncomplicated to examine the physical, mental and personality requirements and rewards of the instruments, one by one.

At the end of the information about each instrument, there is a Suitability Summary.

It is worth filling in all the Suitability Summaries, even if you have already decided in your own mind that the instruments in a particular group are inappropriate.

DO put a cross against any aspect of an instrument which does not suit your child.

DON'T be tempted to put a tick, if you are less than certain it is right.

DON'T WORRY if you feel that you ought to leave some squares blank. For example, it may be difficult to decide on physical feed-back until the child has had the opportunity of holding the instrument and going through the motions of playing. These DON'T KNOWS resolve themselves automatically later on.

THINKING ABOUT THE WOODWIND

The woodwind instruments are all pipes which you blow to play tunes. Flute, oboe and clarinet are high or treble instruments; the bassoon is a low, bass instrument. The saxophones and recorders range from high to low.

Parents know that most modern children want quick results. In musical terms, today's children want to make a nice sound and be able to play tunes in a few months.

The flute and clarinet figure on more short lists than any other instruments because they (and, for older children, the saxophones, too) give this kind of rapid achievement. The oboe and bassoon do not.

The woodwind instruments play only one note at a time. So the written music is neither difficult to read, nor is a good memory required. These instruments do so much of the work of making the sound that no especial musicality or even good sense of pitch is required. Many children who cannot sing a tune perfectly can learn to play a flute or clarinet quite well.

Little parental involvement is called for by children learning to play these instruments, apart from natural encouragement and support.

All this group of instruments were, as the name tells us, originally made of wood and powered by wind, i.e. the controlled breath of the player. Today, oboes, clarinets and bassoons are still made of wood or plastic, but most flutes are now made of metal. The saxophones are late-comers to the woodwind family and have always been made of brass. Piccolo, cor anglais, E Flat clarinet, bass clarinet and contra bassoon also belong to the woodwind but are not for beginners. Fifes and penny whistles, etc. also belong to this group.

Although these instruments are grouped together for convenience, the 'feed-back' of playing them differs considerably. There is little similarity between the feeling of blowing over the open hole of a flute and forcing air through the narrow reed of the oboe; or between the way in which the lips are folded tightly over the teeth to grip the oboe reed and the manner in which the clarinet mouthpiece is thrust right into the mouth. Few children will be attracted equally to flute and clarinet; if they really like one, they won't like the other very much. Very few children will want to play the oboe or the bassoon.

Children who have enjoyed playing the recorder either in school or at home are naturally attracted, as they grow older and bigger, to the apparently similar instruments in the wood-wind group. Parents should bear in mind that learning the recorder is an excellent training for any instrument. The fact that a child has enjoyed the recorder when young should not restrict the choice of the second instrument only to the woodwind family, even though the flute or the clarinet will almost certainly appear on that child's short list.

Children today spend a lot of time sitting in school, in vehicles, watching television and so on. Playing a wood-wind or a brass instrument expresses some of the otherwise unused physical energy, whilst not demanding a great deal of sheer strength.

As to price, oboes and saxophones may seem expensive and bassoons *are* very expensive, but beginners' flutes and clarinets cost little more than a teenager's bicycle and have the advantage that, like all instruments, they hold their value well for possible resale or trade-in.

Flute

Children like the sound of the flute, the notes first learned lying in the register of a ten-year-old's voice. It is an instrument designed to play tunes on. Playing tunes, or singing them, is the way in which a child naturally expresses his or her musical instincts. Hence, the appeal of the flute.

Flutes of one kind or another have been used for playing tunes for many thousands of years, all over the world. The orchestral flute, as we know it, is a reedless instrument, held horizontal to the right side of the body. Sound is produced by pursing the lips and blowing a controlled stream of air across the open hole of the head-joint – rather like blowing over a pen-top or the head of a milk bottle. This sounds – and is – simple, but some children do not have the necessary lip control to do it. The flute is not for them.

The keywork on a modern flute may look complicated, but the golden rule with instruments is: *the more complicated they are as machines, the easier they are to play.* (A very simple instrument like the violin leaves all the work to the player, while the mechanically more complicated flute or clarinet does much of the work for you, so progress in learning can be rapid.)

Within weeks, a beginner can progress from playing

notes, and the satisfaction of producing a musical sound, to playing simple tunes from ear and written music.

The flute comes into three pieces and fits into a small carrying case. It is easily put together and can be played and practised anywhere, better standing than seated.

Fingering is similar to that for the recorder, which gets recorder-players off to a flying start!

Physical Suitability

Many young children are attracted to the flute and want to begin learning it long before their bodies are ready. Unlike the violin or the guitar, which are available in small sizes for beginners, it is not possible to make a reduced-sized wind instrument, for technical reasons. (The piccolo is not a small-size flute; it is a different instrument.) Therefore, the body of a child playing the flute has to do the same work as that of an adult flautist, for whose much larger body the instrument was designed.

A single look at most young children playing the flute demonstrates the problem: in order to reduce the distance which the left arm has to stretch, the flute is not held horizontal, as it should be. This in turn means that the neck has to be twisted and the head held crooked in order to keep the lips at right angles to the flute.

The 'right age to begin playing the flute' is when the child can stand upright, with the neck straight, and hold the flute horizontal, with the left arm comfortably stretched across the chest. As long as a child has to twist the head and neck in order to reduce the left-arm stretch, he or she is too small to start playing the flute.

Because there is no reed on the flute to produce the basic sound, the shape of the lips is very important. Thick lips or very thin lips are not advised. Large upper front teeth are a handicap.

There is little obvious feed-back when trying out the flute in a music shop. The feed-back from playing comes after a few minutes of blowing: the flute uses so much air that playing it is like continuously blowing up balloons – it can make you very dizzy and even nauseated. Girls who like the feeling of moving to music, in dance or ballet, feel good playing the flute in a standing position, which is how it should always be practised.

The flute is the only instrument held far out to the side of the body. It is so designed that it can only be held to the right. This makes it a difficult instrument for complete left-handers who have an insufficient awareness of what is going on on the right side of their bodies.

The player cannot see his or her fingers whilst playing; because there is no visual check on what the fingers are doing and because playing the flute uses all eight fingers and the left thumb, a child with any problem or difficulty in controlling and co-ordinating the fingers will not be happy on the flute.

Mental Suitability

The flute suits a wide range of mental ability: comparatively slow learners happily spend months, even years, learning to play simple tunes beautifully; quick learners race ahead, extending technique, increasing speed and progressing to increasingly difficult studies and repertoire.

Flute music is easy to read, so flute-players do not need particularly good memories.

Personality Suitability

Shy or lonely children (who enjoy their own privacy) adore playing tunes on their flutes day after day, week after week.

But quietly sociable children are equally happy to find that, after about a year of learning properly, they can make music together with their friends in self-organized groups and be welcome in almost every kind of supervised music-making ensembles, orchestras and bands of all kinds.

Probably the only kind of child who can find no satisfaction on this instrument is the aggressive or dominant child who needs to expend more energy and produce more noise than the flute will allow.

SUITABILITY SUMMARY	✓ OR ✗
Physical	
Mental	
Personality	

Clarinet

At a casual glance, the clarinet may look similar to the recorder. In fact, it is very different in almost every respect.

To produce a sound on the recorder, you place the mouthpiece between your lips and simply blow into it. On the clarinet, the sound is produced by the player thrusting the mouthpiece inside the mouth and holding it with the front upper teeth while blowing to vibrate the wide reed which is clamped to the mouthpiece. This is similar to the way in which children make a squeaky noise by vibrating a blade of grass stretched between the thumbs.

Vibrating the clarinet reed can produce a surprising volume of sound for little effort. However, the vibration of the reed inside the mouth produces a very strong feed-back of which the player cannot be unaware.

Many boys are drawn to the instrument because it can make such a 'big sound' and also because the notes first learnt correspond to the slightly lower register of a boy's voice.

Its design gives the clarinet a great range of notes, which enables it to play, and be a solo instrument in, many kinds of music.

Alone among the woodwind, the clarinet has its own system of fingering, but this is not a problem, except initially for children who have played the recorder previously. (All the other woodwind use a modified system of recorder fingering.)

Most children find it easy to produce a sound on the clarinet, find the fingering logical and are reassured by being able to see their hands whilst playing.

Parents are amazed how quickly their children can make progress on this instrument. Within a few weeks, they can play tunes. Within months, they are ready to join a school band or orchestra.

Physical Suitability

To play the clarinet, the player inserts the mouthpiece, to which the reed is fastened, right into the mouth. Some children find the sensation of the reed vibrating inside the mouth very satisfying; for others, it is like trying to play a dentist's drill!

It is easier to make a sound on the clarinet than on the flute, for the reed does some of the work for you. Strong front teeth which would be a nuisance on the flute are a positive advantage on the clarinet.

The playing position is comfortable for most nine- or ten-year-olds, with the hands clearly in view in front of the body, especially on the new C and Kinder E Flat models.

Make sure that (a) fingers can span the distance between the keys, which is greater than on the flute, (b) pads of the fingertips are broad enough to cover the open-hole keys.

Mental Suitability

Quick learners and impatient children enjoy the rapidity of progress on the clarinet.

The music is not difficult to read but the great range of

the instrument means that it is harder to read and play clarinet music than music for flute or oboe.

Also, because each note has its own fingering on the clarinet (for technical reasons), it demands a higher degree of finger co-ordination and control. Boys with a passion for model-making and taking things to pieces have developed this set of skills better than most girls.

Advanced clarinet-playing can be stimulating for a mentally agile child as it involves the use of two instruments and sometimes transposition.

Personality Suitability

Clarinet children tend to have several different hobbies or interests and flit from one to another. They are bright and alert, whereas a flute child may seem dreamy and forgetful.

The clarinet tends to suit sociable children rather than those who want to play on their own. After acquiring a basic competence on the instrument, most clarinettists become bored with their own company and look forward to the prospect of playing with others in orchestras, bands or clarinet choirs.

SUITABILITY SUMMARY	✓ OR ✗
Physical	
Mental	
Personality	

Saxophones

These instruments are often overlooked by parents, yet for children who do not like classical music and do not want to play in formal orchestras or chamber groups they have a lot to offer.

There are four different saxophones: soprano, alto, tenor and baritone (rather like the four different recorders). Older children with a good sense of rhythm can get a lot of fun from the alto or tenor sax.

Of all instruments, the saxophones come closest to the sound of the human voice – not the high, piping voice of a little child, maybe, but certainly from early adolescence onwards. Boys as their voices break and girls who grow tall tend to find that they outgrow any natural desire to make the clean treble sound of a recorder or flute but are attracted to the lower, throaty sound of the alto and tenor saxes. Conversely, few young children or small-bodied girls will naturally like the sound of these instruments.

The fingering is similar to that for recorder, flute and oboe. Thus, children who want to change from these other woodwind instruments, transfer happily and quickly to the sax, feeling that what they have previously learnt has not been wasted. The freedom available to sax-players improvising in jazz and dance bands appeals to teenagers who want to express their personalities or be more 'creative' than is possible playing written music in an orchestra.

Saxophones are expensive – around twice the cost of a flute or clarinet.

Physical Suitability

Few children start to play the saxes before the age of twelve or thirteen. The playing position is quite comfortable by this age, with the weight of the instrument (saxophones are heavy!) largely borne by the sling around the player's neck. Although much larger than flutes, oboes and clarinets, the saxophones, being of recent invention, are designed to be easier to operate. No great hand-stretches are involved, but, as hands are out of sight – except on the soprano sax which is small enough to be held in front of the body – reasonable finger co-ordination is called for.

The large mouthpiece inserted into the player's mouth produces a vibration feed-back similar to that of the clarinet and calls for strong or large teeth and generous lips.

Mental Suitability

Quick results for all! Much easier to learn than flute or clarinet, the sax is easy to play and the music not difficult to read. Satisfying progress is made without much practising.

Personality Suitability

These instruments suit children who may have been labelled 'casual' or 'unable to concentrate' but are by no means dull. Happy, well-balanced gregarious players, who do not want a close relationship with a teacher, find the saxes an ideal way of getting out into the world and making music with friends – and making friends with music.

Adolescents who already play one or more classical instruments (such as piano and violin) are often attracted to the sax because it promises such relief from the inhibitions of written music and formal style. For them, the sax is a fun instrument: easy to learn, loud – and designed for the delicious freedom of improvisation.

SUITABILITY SUMMARY	✓ OR ✗
Physical	
Mental	
Personality	

Oboe

In the hands of an outstanding professional musician play-ing chamber or orchestral music, the oboe can sound exquisite. Played by most children who are learning, the sound is unpleasing and rasping, which offers little en-couragement to the player or to other members of the family within earshot. If your child is vaguely thinking about the oboe, or the school is trying to persuade him or her to take it up and play in the orchestra, there is only one word of advice: Don't!

The only children who can enjoy learning this instrument are those who, for a complex of reasons difficult for the outsider – even a parent – to unravel, simply know a hundred per cent that this is the instrument for them. It is self-selecting in every sense, usually by children of about twelve or thirteen who have learnt to read music on a previous instrument and like the sound or the idea of playing in the woodwind section of an orchestra sufficiently to justify the long devotion and hard practice necessary to make any progress.

Fingering is similar to that of the recorder and flute, but the lip technique is extremely difficult to acquire.

Physical Suitability

The most important physical requirement is the shape of the lips: they must be thin and tight, capable of being folded over the teeth to grip the narrow reed which is inserted into the mouth. The vibration of the reed within the mouth when playing is a feeling which some children like; others it makes squeamish.

The aperture between the two pieces of reed is so tight that the player has to *force* the breath through. Children may experience headaches from the back-pressure which this causes, even in a healthy teenager.

Not an instrument for frail children: the breath control is harder for the oboe than for any other wind instrument and so it must not be attempted unless the child is physically fit, even athletic – and the older the better. The oboe should never be played or even practised by any adolescent with a head-cold, respiratory or virus infection. The inter-cranial pressure can spread the infection into the eyes and the brain causing complications and even disability.

Mental Suitability

Impossible to generalize! There are no quick results, but any *determined* learner with the *sheer willpower* to succeed and the necessary motivation can make progress.

Personality Suitability

The oboe is not for generous extroverts; determined, tight-lipped, stubborn children do best. A strong and close relationship with the teacher is called for in order to make progress. Insecure or intense adolescents often benefit by forming this kind of relationship with an adult outside the family.

Oboists tend not to mix well but to have one or two close friends. Even in an orchestral woodwind section, the oboe-players make a little clan and keep to themselves.

SUITABILITY SUMMARY	✓ OR ✗
Physical	
Mental	
Personality	

Bassoon

Few parents will consider the bassoon. It is a large instrument, not recommended for or chosen by young children. It is very expensive.

The bassoon is the largest woodwind instrument by far. It is nearly five feet long and every foot costs a lot of money. If a child is really determined to play the bassoon and the money simply is not available to hire or buy one, it is worth 'hustling' a little, going from school to school and music centre to music centre to find one available on loan. The favour works in both directions: your child has the instrument without crippling the family budget and the school or music centre fills the bassoonist's chair in the orchestra.

To play any bass instrument requires a good ear, to listen to the higher-register instruments and play harmoniously with them.

Usually adolescent children come to the bassoon as a second instrument after first learning to play a self-contained instrument such as the piano. They feel, or a teacher says, that they now need the experience of playing together with others and are ready to enjoy playing harmony rather than tunes.

Physical Suitability

A big and heavy instrument. Although some of the weight is borne by a spike or a sling when playing, few children under thirteen are tall enough, strong enough, have a sufficient finger-span and wide enough fingertips to play it.

The reed is like a very large and thick oboe reed. The player's lips must be folded back to grip it but not as tightly as for the oboe.

Good co-ordination is required as the player can see neither the keys nor his fingers when playing.

Mental Suitability

No special requirements.

Many slow learners are drawn to the warm sound of this very 'human' instrument. The music is comparatively easy to read, but written in bass clef.

Personality Suitability

'Responsive' or 'pleasantly gregarious' are the sort of adjectives that could be used to describe most bassoonists. A quiet sense of humour helps. Indeed, bassoon-players tend to be the practical jokers of the orchestra. No good for playing on one's own, the bassoon is essentially an orchestral instrument.

SUITABILITY SUMMARY	✓ OR ✗
Physical	
Mental	
Personality	

Recorders

The recorders are really a whole sub-group of instruments within the woodwind group. They range from the tiny sopranino, which is very high-sounding, through the descant, treble and tenor recorders to the largest of all: the bass recorder.

Although some schools own the full range, the recorder which is familiar to most children is the descant recorder. It is a simple tube with holes cut in it at precise intervals. Its basic design was evolved tens of thousands of years ago. People all over the world make and play similar simple instruments. A descant recorder is the cheapest proper instrument you can buy.

The recorder is a real instrument, not a toy. Indeed, advanced recorder technique is extremely difficult. As on all simple instruments – the violin is another example – all the work has to be done by the player, with no valves, keys or other mechanical bits and pieces to make things easier. Unfortunately, there are few music teachers who will give lessons in advanced recorder technique. Most children eventually lose interest in the instrument, if for no other reason, than the lack of a progressive course of structured lessons.

If few children can learn to play the recorder to advanced levels, almost all children can benefit from the recorder as a preparatory instrument. It is an excellent way to accustom the child to the basic principles of operating an instrument and reading simple notation. Not all children who learn recorder at school get the benefits, however, because the lessons are almost always group lessons, in which a few children learn the instrument – while the others play 'follow my leader'.

If your child is learning the recorder in group lessons, the recorder can be a very useful indicator for you: as long as the child is happy playing, alone or with friends, the simple repertoire of tunes learnt at school, he or she is not quite ready to start formal lessons on another instrument. The right time to begin proper lessons on a technically more advanced instrument is when the child becomes bored with group lessons, or the technical limitations of the instrument.

Physical Suitability

Most children find holding the recorder comfortable and pleasurable. A child who does not like putting the recorder in the mouth and keeping it there, or who finds the controlled breathing stressful, cannot enjoy the recorder.

The first fingers used are those of the left hand. The physical co-ordination necessary to play left-hand tunes is within the possibilities of most six-year-olds. The problems arise when, after a few months of learning, it is necessary to co-ordinate individual fingers of both hands, sometimes together and sometimes separately. Many children of eight or nine (and many adults) cannot do this.

Compare the physical difficulty of playing the recorder with both hands and the simplicity of playing a brass instrument with three fingers of one hand only.

Little physical energy is required, or can be released, in playing the recorder. Frail children, including those with respiratory problems, can enjoy the satisfaction of making a musical sound with the minimum of physical exertion. Because it does not release much energy, boys tend to 'go off' the recorder earlier than girls.

Mental Suitability

Most children who are ready to go to school can learn to play simple tunes on the descant recorder, using the left hand only at first.

Personality Suitability

Children who enjoy singing derive great pleasure from playing the recorder. Boisterous children find the sound of the instrument, and its music, unsatisfying.

Quietly behaved, gentle children who do well on the descant recorder, move on to the other recorders in junior orchestras, recorder groups and Early Music groups. Here, they can make 'real music' in harmonically structured ensembles.

SUITABILITY SUMMARY	✓ OR ✗
Physical	
Mental	
Personality	

THINKING ABOUT THE BRASS

You may not have thought about a brass instrument, yet the brass are the instruments of tomorrow for the vast majority of children.

The advantages of the brass are many:

- any child who can sing or whistle a tune from memory can learn to play a brass instrument;
- beginners' instruments are cheap to buy and are often borrowed free of charge from local bands;
- they are robust and need little looking after apart from cleaning and occasional oiling of the moving parts;
- they last for years and keep their value well for resale;
- playing most of these instruments uses only three fingers of the right hand, unlike the piano, or the clarinet, for example, which requires precise co-ordination of all ten digits. Only *very* left-handed children may find this a problem;
- the cost of learning need not be high, for the brass instruments are usually taught in group situations and through bands, rather than by private individual lessons;

- because the whole point of learning a brass instrument is to play it in a band, the instrument automatically gives the child an outgoing, sociable activity – a sort of musical youth club to belong to;
- playing a brass instrument releases a lot of energy otherwise pent up in the telly-addicted child – after a good session with the rest of the band, you feel good and glowing with health, like after a yoga session or a good game of football;
- there is a brass instrument for every physical build from the small and light cornet to the massive tuba or bass – playing the brass builds a healthy body;
- learning the brass can embrace every kind of mentality: quick and brilliant learners have the endless and difficult repertoire of the solo cornet; slow learners, and those who are happy plodding away at the back, are content to play with the other easygoing members of the tuba or bass section;
- thanks to the brass-band movement, every kind of music is arranged for brass instruments to play, which means that, whatever kind of music your child prefers, he or she can easily find it arranged for brass – from Early Music through classical and jazz to modern pop and light music.

There are three general disadvantages:

- some children do not like the physical feed-back of vibrating the lips against the mouthpiece and pushing lungfuls of air through the instrument;
- genuinely solitary children cannot take the close physical and emotional relationship in a band (and only the French horn offers satisfaction to the lone learner);

- you must have a local junior band or orchestra or group to play in.

While a parent may think of the brass as one section of a symphony orchestra, modern children are more likely to picture a brass instrument as belonging to a brass or dance band. It is worth distinguishing which brass instruments are played in orchestras and which in brass bands, since you may live in an area which has school orchestras and not bands, or vice versa, and there is no point learning a brass instrument if you cannot get together with others to play it.

Some of the orchestral brass sections comprise, from small and high-sounding to large and low-sounding: trumpet, French horn, trombone, tuba. In junior orchestras, cornets sometimes play the trumpet part.

A brass band is like a choir. Instead of having voices, it has the smaller, high-sounding instruments to play the tunes, middle-sized and middle-sounding instruments to provide harmony and the large bass instruments for the solid bottom of the sound. From high to low, they are: cornet (which has most of the tunes), tenor horn and baritone, trombone, euphonium, E Flat and B Flat basses.

Also belonging to the brass, but rarely played as first instruments by children, are post horn, coach horn, piccolo trumpet, flugel horn.

The bugle is a marvellous starter instrument for children not quite old enough to begin one of the valved instruments. It is not a progressive instrument because its simple construction restricts it to only five notes, but young children with an urge to try a brass instrument get a lot of fun out of playing in a marching band for a year or so. This is not a waste, for they learn to train both lip and ear, the two essentials for any serious brass instrument – and they usually have a very good time belonging to their first band.

What a variety to choose from! Most short lists of children over eight or nine will include one of the brass instruments, unless one of the three disadvantages rules otherwise.

Cornet

Unless you know about brass bands, you may not even consider the cornet – thinking wrongly that it is just another kind of trumpet.

It is much more than that. The cornet is fun. It is a splendid instrument for children aged eight upwards to learn. It has a pleasing sound, more gentle than the trumpet, is good for playing tunes on and, because it is not physically very hard work to play, is often used as a preparatory instrument for young children who want to learn any of the other brass instruments.

The cornet is not just a preparatory instrument. It is also the lead instrument of the brass band, as important as the trumpet in a dance band or the first violins in an orchestra.

Brass bands generally are run by energetic, generous people. Players themselves, their main concern is to encourage and help the next generation of players. It is the rule, rather than the exception, that a band will lend an instrument free of charge to a young learner. Most learning is done in rehearsals and band practices rather than in individual lessons. In a junior band, beginners are welcome to sit in on the third cornet part, playing one or two notes.

Physical Suitability

The cornet is light to hold and play. The hands are kept comfortably close to the body. Although looking a little like a short, curly trumpet on the outside, the internal design of the cornet is different, requiring much less 'puff'.

Asthmatic or bronchial children can benefit greatly from the cornet. Playing it is for them a gentle exercise which builds, rather than strains, the body. Also, they are often very happy to find at last a sociable group activity in which they can take part.

Many a healthy and boisterous seven-year-old may have sufficient energy to blow the cornet, but it is a good idea to wait until the second teeth are firm in the gums before starting to learn properly.

Only three fingers of the right hand are used to operate the valves. Most children find this no problem. Any child who likes the physical feed-back of vibrating the lips and blowing will naturally develop the necessary lip co-ordination. Children who do not like this physical feed-back will never be happy on a brass instrument.

Mental Suitability

An instrument for both tortoises and hares! The tortoises are happy staying in third and second cornet sections; ambitious hares can race through the stages of technique to the more demanding solo parts.

Personality Suitability

Most sociable children can enjoy the cornet. The easygoing ones are happy to plod away with the thirds; the aggressive, and dominant or ambitious child (who may later transfer to the trumpet) can find an outlet for his energies in the nervy tension of the solo cornet.

Joining a junior band is an excellent activity for the child who wants to feel independent of the family.

SUITABILITY SUMMARY	✓ OR ✗
Physical	
Mental	
Personality	

Trumpet

The trumpet is a powerful, aggressive instrument for out-going, dominant and physically strong children.

All brass instruments are sounded in the same way: the player purses his lips against the mouthpiece and blows a raspberry. This basic sound is then modulated by the size and shape of the instrument – much as the old-fashioned gramophone horn amplified the scratching of the needle on the surface of the record. Distinct notes are produced by tightening and slackening the lips, and by the player depressing one or more valves, or using the slide on the trombone.

The hole in a trumpet mouthpiece is very small, which makes it hard work to force much air through it. At the same time, the instrument is not large and therefore not very efficient at amplifying the sound. To compensate, the player has to strain to force enough air into the instrument. The higher you play, the greater the strain.

It is possible, of course, to play quietly on the trumpet. Indeed, orchestral trumpeters spend most of their time doing so, but that is not the kind of trumpet-playing which attracts many children to the instrument.

Few children will get much satisfaction from learning and playing the trumpet on their own. Trumpeters want to play with, and dominate, others. A junior orchestra gives no outlet for this, so it is important to make sure that the young trumpet-player can find a local junior dance band, show band, big band or concert band to play in. Remember that the local brass band probably cannot help here (because there are no trumpets in brass bands), although some junior brass bands allow young trumpeters to 'sit in' in the cornet sections.

Physical Suitability

You need energy to play the trumpet – the kind of short-burst energy which makes a football or netball centre-forward. Sheer size is not important. Many children who are a little small for their age feel especially good making a big sound on the trumpet.

The usual age to begin is about ten or eleven. Children starting the trumpet earlier, before teeth and gums are firm, risk deforming their mouths.

Mental Suitability

You must be alert to play the trumpet: the music has more notes to read and play than the other brass parts. Also, the trumpet is always audible, so any mistakes are obvious to all the other players.

Personality Suitability

The trumpet is a dominant, or solo, instrument suitable for the *prima donna* temperament. The trumpeter is an independent boy or girl who wants to dominate the sound of the group. He or she has the nerve to play long solos, aiming for success, but also risking failure in front of classmates and friends. This characteristic tends to go with 'nervous energy' found in the kind of child who will force him- or herself to go one step further than is safe.

Trumpeters are individualists, who do not belong to the group, but get along well enough with other children – providing they have their full share of the limelight.

SUITABILITY SUMMARY	✓ OR ✗
Physical	
Mental	
Personality	

Tenor Horn and Baritone

These instruments, which look like small tubas, are found only in bands. The tenor horn is smaller and light to hold and play; the baritone is slightly larger and sounds lower.

Learning tenor horn or baritone is a good preparation for the larger and lower brass and the technically more demanding French horn and flugel horn.

Physical Suitability

These instruments are light and comfortable for boys and girls from nine upwards to hold and play.

These horns demand least energy of all the brass. A little puff into the eggcup-size mouthpiece goes a long way in producing that mellow and gentle sound which is the characteristic of these instruments.

Mental Suitability

The music is not difficult to read. Other players in the section tend to be helpful, so that even children who are not thought of as bright in school make progress and find they are good at something – and as important as anyone else in the band.

Personality Suitability

These instruments are very satisfying for gentle children who do not want to dominate or play the tune, but are peaceful, feeling that they belong to a group. They are easy-going, responsive children who like being 'in the middle of things' – like the viola-players in the orchestra.

Responsible and never 'bossy', they are often asked to become organizers, e.g. the librarian who looks after the band's music, or the band secretary who arranges rehearsals, etc.

SUITABILITY SUMMARY	✓ OR ✗
Physical	
Mental	
Personality	

Trombone

The trombone is different from all the other brass. The others are semi-machines and have valves to help find different notes. On the trombone, as on the violin, the player has to form each note, adjusting the position of the slide microscopically to give exactly the 'shape' of note he wants. This is very satisfying to an artistic or creative child.

Pushing down the valves of the other brass instruments (their springs push them back up) is a fairly jerky and mechanical exercise, whereas the flowing movements of the trombonist's right arm and wrist are a pleasure for the kind of children who want to move in sympathy with music.

It is a lyrical instrument: children who enjoy singing and the feeling of making music with their own vocal chords and lungs, yet who like the feed-back of lips vibrating against mouthpiece, will almost always opt for the trombone – as the brass instrument on which you come nearest to singing.

Also, singers have an important advantage. A keen sense of pitch is vital. There are no valves to determine the pitch of the sound mechanically. Therefore, the trombonist must constantly listen to his own sound, control it, monitor the sound of the other players, and adjust his intonation to theirs.

Few parents will be able to assess a child's sense of pitch sufficiently well, but any music teacher can give your child a series of tests, such as the Bentley tests, which tell you whether your child has a sufficiently good ear to play the trombone.

Younger children are naturally attracted to the higher-pitched instruments, which sound roughly in the same register as their own voices. Teenagers, especially boys whose voices break early and tall girls who have deeper voices than some of their shorter friends, are similarly attracted by the tenor register of the trombone.

Physical Suitability

Playing the trombone gives no outlet for the angry energy which makes a trumpeter. The instrument suits physically well-balanced children with the kind of controlled energy which makes good cricketers, ice-skaters or athletes. Although the trombone is very long, it is much lighter to hold and play than you might think.

It is usual to begin learning at about eleven or twelve. Younger children have a problem coping with the right-arm stretches.

The mouthpiece is very much larger than on the cornet or trumpet, requiring more fleshy lips.

This is the only wind instrument (that term embraces both woodwind and brass) which is possible for children with very poor finger control. The fingers do nothing except support the instrument and move the slide in and out.

Mental Suitability

In a brass band, the trombonist's role is not very demanding. All his music is written in treble clef and he spends his time supplying harmonies to the higher-sounding instruments. In the orchestra, he has to use his brain more, as the parts may be written in any of three clefs (due to the great range of the instrument). However, this is the most versatile of the brass, and the adolescent player who is bored with his orchestral or band role can branch out, according to his musical preferences, into dance bands, big bands, concert bands; he can seek the freedom of improvising in jazz groups or the serious introspection of brass chamber music. Most trombonists are bright and quick-witted and play more than one kind of music with equal pleasure. They are good 'all-rounders'.

Personality Suitability

Because each note is 'shaped' by the player, this is the brass instrument most fulfilling for artistic children who need to feel they are making the sound. Particularly satisfying for the adolescent who wants to express his or her personality playing in jazz bands or other improvising situations.

Most children who succeed on the trombone are quietly sociable, sensitive and artistic.

SUITABILITY SUMMARY	✓ OR ✗
Physical	
Mental	
Personality	

Euphonium

The euphonium looks like an overgrown baritone or a stunted tuba. It is more than that, having a soulful quality all of its own. The thought of one of these large instruments being played in a bedroom upstairs while other members of the family have to concentrate on homework or listen to their own music might seem frightening, but the reality is that the sound is quite peaceful and much less disturbing and penetrating than that of the smaller, high-pitched instruments.

The name, euphonium, means sweet-sounding. Today, we expect only high or very loud instruments to play tunes, but in the brass band, the euphonium is the second most important instrument after the cornet. It has its bass, harmonic role but is also a featured solo instrument in almost every concert.

Physical Suitability

This is an instrument to which children move on from tenor horn or baritone horn as they grow bigger and can cope with its size and the extra puff needed.

Mental Suitability

The euphonium suits quietly intelligent children who have a

sense of melody and like to feel that they can play tunes on their instrument, yet do not have the aggression necessary for, and are not attracted to, a high instrument.

Personality Suitability

Responsive children. There is no room in a band for a euphonium player who brashly plays away without listening to the higher instruments.

SUITABILITY SUMMARY	✓ OR ✗
Physical	
Mental	
Personality	

Tuba, E Flat, B Flat Bass

'Tuba' is the orchestral name; the same instrument in a brass band is called an E Flat (or B Flat) bass. Whatever it is called, it is big! Yet, it takes less energy to play than the tiny piccolo, or the trumpet. This is because of the way in which brass instruments function: you do not have to fill a brass instrument with air from your lungs each time you play a note, so the sheer size of the tuba places no great demand on the strength of the player; rather the reverse, its size acts as an amplifier, like the old-fashioned gramophone horn.

Where the size is a drawback is in carrying it, transporting it on the bus – and finding a place to keep it in the bedroom.

The single tuba-player in an orchestra can get lonely, but playing E Flat or B Flat bass in a brass band, together with the other basses, is great fun.

Physical Suitability

The kind of surplus physical energy that makes a child aggressive is misplaced on these instruments. Many slightly overweight children who do not have a lot of spare energy are very happy on the tuba.

Mental Suitability

You do not need an agile brain. The music is not difficult to read, it is repetitive and you rarely have to play fast. A good sense of rhythm helps a lot and makes playing more pleasurable. The brief solos may not be wildly exciting to listen to, but they are very rewarding to play.

Personality Suitability

Responsible, good-natured boys who are happy belonging to a group can be content in band or orchestra playing what seem like endless oompahs to an outsider. It is a bit like being full-back or goalkeeper on the football pitch – a lot of hanging about, but at times you are vital.

SUITABILITY SUMMARY	✓ OR ✗
Physical	
Mental	
Personality	

French Horn

So far, we have dealt with the brass instruments in order of descending pitch. The French horn is not the lowest-sounding, but has been left until last because it is the most difficult, has little to offer the majority of children and is an exception to most of the generalizations about the brass instruments.

The French horn is not recommended as a first instrument. It is not for fun. It is self-selecting, like the oboe, and appeals to rather similar children.

To produce its distinctive and beautiful sound requires mastery of a technique more difficult than that of any other brass instrument. One position of the player's fingers on the three rotary valves can produce up to twenty notes: only an acute sense of pitch enables the player to conjure the right one out of thin air, by lip control alone.

Almost every child who succeeds on this instrument has previously overcome any problems in reading music through learning the piano or another instrument – or through singing – and desperately wants to play this instrument above all others.

Parental help and encouragement is needed, especially in the early stages. Because the French horn is an orchestral, not a brass-band instrument, the child learning has none of that friendly help, encouragement and boosting of morale that comes naturally to other brass learners at their weekly band practice.

French horns are very expensive to buy. Although it is possible to begin with small-group instruction, individual lessons swiftly become necessary for any real progress to be made.

Physical Suitability

Thin to medium lips are called for by the mouthpiece. The small bore through which the air has to be directed produces back-pressure which can cause headaches and dizziness even in quite mature learners. Twelve or thirteen is the conventional starting age.

The French horn is the only brass instrument which develops finger co-ordination for the left hand; the right hand is thrust into the bell to support the weight of the instrument and to help modify the sound.

Mental Suitability

You can never relax playing the French horn; each note must be *achieved*; there is no letting up.

Any child with a good enough ear and the necessary lip control can succeed. Whether he or she does depends on willpower and self-discipline as well as intelligence, which is needed because the horn is a transposing instrument – indeed, a mental-arithmetic brain helps.

Personality Suitability

French horn children are not gregarious. Not for them the happy, club-like atmosphere of a brass band. They prefer to relate to small groups and usually have just one or two close friends. The horn-players in an orchestra or concert band make a definite clique and do not mix much even with the other members of the brass section.

Only conscientious, intense children, who have an inner need to work hard and apply themselves over a long period, sustain progress on this instrument. Happier, more easygoing children may – if they have a good ear – begin apparently quite well but give up after reaching the stage of playing a few tunes with the school band, defeated by the difficulties of playing the high and low notes.

The playing position seems to suit, and even comfort, children who feel, rightly or wrongly, that they do not get enough attention at home or school: middle children, for example. With excellent justification, they feel special about playing the horn, for only a very unusual child can.

They may be children who feel that they have under-achieved themselves. They like the noble shape of the French horn, compared with the simple robustness of the other brass instruments. They are naturally possessive of their intricate and expensive instrument and proud to carry it about.

This is probably the only brass instrument which will be practised for endless hours in the privacy of the bedroom. The child who truly wants to be and play alone, is eventually rewarded by an extensive repertoire of music which can be played and practised alone. This is particularly important for a child who for geographical, social or any other reasons cannot go out and play in groups or orchestras.

Children who need the solace of classical music will find a greater potential on this instrument than the other brass.

SUITABILITY SUMMARY	✓ OR ✗
Physical	
Mental	
Personality	

THINKING ABOUT THE STRINGS

All the instruments we have looked at so far have one important characteristic in common: the woodwind and brass instruments are for children who have physical energy to use up, by blowing.

Violin, viola and cello are for children with *mental energy* to spare, mental energy which is not absorbed by school, homework, hobbies, etc.

With the sole exception of the trombone, the 'machinery' of woodwind and brass instruments is quite complicated in order to make them easy to play. The construction of the stringed instruments is very simple and they are very difficult to play. Hence the requirement of mental energy.

There never were any easy satisfactions or quick results on the stringed instruments. A couple of generations ago this did not matter, for children were disciplined to work for two or three years at something without expecting any results. Such children could settle down and learn a stringed instrument. Modern children live at a quicker pace and cannot easily defer satisfaction. Most of them *need* the quick results of woodwind and brass.

Unless your child is exceptionally conscientious and

patient, it is unlikely that he or she will continue studying a stringed instrument to the point of any real achievement, which takes not months but *several years*.

The child for whom the strings are open to consideration must have spare mental energy, be measurably more musical than most co-evals, have a good sense of pitch, be drawn to classical music, and be very conscientious. For such a child, playing a stringed instrument will become a joy, an enrichment and a source of lifelong spiritual uplift.

Violin

The violin is a hollow box, made of thin, resonant wood, which amplifies the vibration of one or more of the four tensed strings. The player has to make the strings vibrate by scraping sticky horsehair across them.

If that sounds to you like a difficult way of making music, then you are one step along the path to understanding why learning the violin is immensely hard and demands years of dedicated work.

A very good sense of pitch is required. The player makes and shapes each note by 'stopping' the strings with the left hand and bowing or plucking with the right. There are no valves, frets, keys or other mechanical devices to help. You need a good ear not only to play the violin, but even to adjust the four strings for each practice session.

Many teachers insist that the parents of young children accompany them to the weekly lessons and take notes in order to supervise the daily practice. This amount of parental involvement, which cannot be skimped, is certainly usual, if not vital for the young learner to succeed.

The violin is the smallest and highest-sounding of the stringed instruments and therefore the one of which the *sound* is most acceptable to young children. It is also the one most commonly available to children as a learning instrument.

The saxophone, fun and *easy* to play after learning recorder

CLOCKWISE FROM TOP
The bass guitar, passport to a rock group or band
The trumpet requires physical energy and a solo temperament
The button accordion, great fun for the sociable adolescent

A good position on the flute, with neck straight and instrument nearly horizontal

A good example . . . of bad matching!

CLOCKWISE FROM TOP LEFT

Not a toy, the recorder is a wonderful preparatory instrument

The treble recorder, an underrated instrument for older children

Family music-making on flute, clarinet and recorders

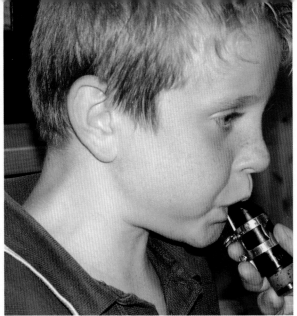

Trying the clarinet reed: does it feel nice or like a dentist's drill?

Quick learners enjoy the speed of progress on the clarinet

A trombonist is welcome in orchestras and bands of *all* kinds

The drumkit, wonderful therapy for a hyperactive child

The piano does not demand physical energy

CLOCKWISE FROM TOP
A musician's daughter with a perfect position on the violin
The cello, an excellent second instrument
The side-drum, as rewarding for the right child as cornet or flute

Progress on the piano is achieved by steady application over many years

Violins are made in three-quarter size, half-size, quarter-size and even one-eighth size, so that there is never a problem in finding an instrument the right size for a child – even from age three upwards. (When buying a small-size violin, you need also a small-size bow to match.)

When assessing the suitability of the violin for your child, it is not important that he or she can hold a small-size fiddle and look comfortable. Rather, think in terms of whether his or her brain is overburdened from coping with school, or with new subjects at school. If in doubt, wait, for there is never any reason to hurry a child into learning an instrument.

Physical Suitability

The instrument suits the light and wiry gymnast or dancer. It is practised standing, which is an exercise in balance for the whole body. It is usually begun by children between the ages of seven and ten on small-size instruments.

The delicate precision required of the player's left hand makes the violin inadvisable for a *heavily* right-handed child. Conversely, most left-handed children can cope with the instrument strung normally.

It is a common misconception among non-players that the violin is supported by the left hand. In fact, the left hand must be free of any weight if it is to do its job of stopping the strings delicately and precisely. The instrument is supported by being gripped between the player's chin and collarbone. Thus, the vibration of the instrument when being played – which is not discernible to an observer, who only *hears* the acoustically transmitted sound – passes by bone-conduction through the child's body directly to the brain. Many children find this vibration unpleasant, even painful. For some children with hearing problems, it can actually be dangerous.

The child who is 'right' on the violin is one who finds this bone-conducted vibration positively pleasant and comforting, often a child who for years carried around a favourite toy or a soft blanket as a comforter.

The other form of feed-back from playing the violin is the feeling of 'moving with the music' as you play. The well-taught child feels the music throughout the whole body. This sensation is particularly satisfying to girls who adore ballet.

Mental Suitability

Most children who make progress on the violin combine intelligence with sensitivity, a good sense of pitch *and a very high degree of conscientiousness.* Parents may wonder why an obviously bright child who learnt to read and write easily, does well at school and is articulate and socially competent, fails to make progress on the violin and gives up, while apparently less intelligent friends carry on and make progress. The answer is usually that the bright child has found everything too easy and never learnt to apply himself. Without conscientious application, sustained progress on the violin is not possible.

Personality Suitability

The stringed instruments offer no outlet for boisterousness or exuberance. They suit quietly behaved children, the sort who are quite happy reading in the bedroom or playing with one or two close friends. Even the string-players in an orchestra make only one or two friends; they do not mix with all fifty other members of the strings sections. The paradox is that they must be able to accept that their principal function as players is to contribute to a corporate sound: the individual string-player is rarely heard alone.

The only child is often drawn to, and does well on, the violin. This is partly because parents spend more time with only children and wish to be involved with their personal development, but also because these children are used to being with, and relating to, adults. Thus, they have the ability to form, and benefit from, a close relationship with the teacher, a *sine qua non* of learning the instrument.

SUITABILITY SUMMARY	✓ OR ✗
Physical	
Mental	
Personality	

Viola

The viola is a larger version of the violin, similarly strung, but sounding lower in quality of tone.

If we compare the stringed instruments to a choir, the violins are like the treble voices singing most of the tunes, cellos and double basses are like bass voices providing the solid bottom of the sound and the violas fill the middle.

The viola is rarely the first instrument learnt by a child. Most viola-players have transferred from the violin or another instrument at about twelve or thirteen. Some prefer the lower sound. Others who have progressed reasonably but unexcitingly on the violin opt for the easier music given to the viola (which does not take up so much time to learn, yet still allows them to enjoy playing in the orchestra). Some boys change when their voices break, preferring an instrument whose register is closer to the sound of their adolescent voices.

Physical Suitability

The viola looks little bigger than a full-size violin, but those few extra inches of length make it *uncomfortable even for many adults* whose left arms are not long enough. The fingers of the left hand have a much wider and more difficult span than on the violin.

Mental Suitability

Similar to that for the violin, but playing viola parts in the orchestra is less demanding than playing the violin.

Personality Suitability

Responsible children who want to contribute to a group endeavour and like classical music find this instrument and its music very peaceful.

SUITABILITY SUMMARY	✓ OR ✗
Physical	
Mental	
Personality	

Cello

Few parents think of the cello as a musical possibility for their children, yet, if there is such a thing as a stringed instrument which is fun for beginners, this is it. Most school orchestras are short of cellists so any reasonable-standard young player is wanted.

There are three very different reasons for considering the cello:

- At one level, a surprisingly large number of children who have the necessary sense of pitch can become good enough to play the cello to a sufficiently good standard to combine with the higher-pitched strings; the parts are simpler to read, the playing position is easier and the initial sound is not discouraging, as it is on the violin.
- Advanced cello technique required by the concerto soloist or in a string quartet is another matter. It calls for the same degree of applied intelligence and sustained hard work as the violin, and offers similar rewards.
- The third reason is as a 'second study'. Children already learning the solitary instruments such as piano, organ or guitar often benefit greatly by having to relate to others both socially and musically in orchestras. The cello makes an excellent second instrument in such cases,

giving both the feeling of playing a stringed instrument and the experience of orchestral music-making, yet not demanding too much extra practising.

A student cello can be hard to come by, especially in the smaller sizes, and will cost three or four times as much as an equivalent-quality violin. A hard case is a good investment, as cellos are easily damaged.

Physical Suitability

The playing position is natural and, unlike that for violin or viola, does not have to be learnt. The weight of the cello is borne by the spike which rests on the floor. Playing the instrument is pleasantly energetic.

Quarter-, half- and three-quarter-size instruments can be found for children from seven onwards, but despite this the cello is not a satisfactory instrument for children of small or below-average build. The left-hand stretches require large hands. Also, the instrument is quite big and heavy to carry about. Few children under thirteen will be able to cope with a full-size cello.

Mental Suitability

At whatever level the cello is played, it suits a quiet and reflective intelligence.

To progress beyond the level of junior orchestra calls for conscientiousness and sustained hard work. The reward to the child who puts in the necessary years of study is a lifetime of music to play: an inexhaustible repertoire of orchestral, chamber and solo music.

Personality Suitability

Few young or small children are naturally attracted to a

low-sounding instrument like the cello. Children with slightly low-pitched voices, children with larger-than-average chest cavities, children with big hands and long arms – all these find a difficult-to-describe satisfaction when trying the cello. It just 'feels right'.

Often these children are shy; for them the hidden reward of playing the cello is the quiet and unstressful sociability enjoyed by cellists in group music-making: rarely in the limelight but always respected.

SUITABILITY SUMMARY	✓ OR ✗
Physical	
Mental	
Personality	

Double Bass

The double bass is the largest and lowest sounding instrument of the orchestra, providing the rhythmic base of the string sound. Even a small-size double bass is a large instrument, standing higher than the child who plays it.

The instrument has its own attractions for children who have had a basis of learning another instrument, can read bass clef easily and who are big.

Physical Suitability

Sheer physical size which makes an overgrown adolescent feel gawky and embarrassed playing a smaller instrument is a positive 'must' for playing the bass. It is important not only to be tall, but also to have large hands with long fingers and a wide finger-span on the left hand. Strength is called for to push that stubby, thick bow across the strings – and to carry the instrument around.

Mental Suitability

There are no great demands. Written bass music is easy to read and play.

Personality Suitability

There is no outlet on the bass for a child who wants to

dominate, but one who is content to play the simple music well and contribute to the overall balance of the string sections of the orchestra is never short of opportunities to play. Older children with an interest in jazz, or who simply like the idea of playing freely with a few friends, find that plucking the bass in a jazz band is strangely fulfilling and creatively satisfying, much more so than the casual listener might think.

SUITABILITY SUMMARY	✓ OR ✗
Physical	
Mental	
Personality	

THINKING ABOUT THE PERCUSSION

The one group of instruments which almost all children have played are those which are hit or shaken: drums, cymbals, triangles, tambourines, wood-blocks – even the baby's rattle.

Most young children enjoy playing with, and on, percussion instruments as an expression of their innate musicality. During Atarah's Band concerts, hundreds of thousands of children accepted our invitation to bring along a percussion instrument and join in with the band. Many adults have been amazed at how seriously and sensitively the children treat their moments of participation in the concert: starting and stopping at the right beat, playing loud and soft as required, playing both simple and complicated rhythms.

School percussion bands can reach high standards and for many children are the high-spot of all their musical experience at school. Playing in these bands is good for a child both musically and socially, yet parents are often baffled as to why there is so little follow-on from the classroom band to a proper course of learning a percussion instrument.

It is precisely because these instruments – or cheap versions of them – are *so familiar* in the primary school, and as toys for little children in the home, that people forget they are real instruments. A proper course of instruction from a qualified percussion teacher can be as rewarding and enriching for the right child as learning the cornet or flute for another kind of child.

There are two kinds of percussion instruments: *the drums and other un-tuned percussion* which cannot play tunes but provide rhythm, and *the tuned percussion*, such as xylophones, chime bars, glockenspiels, on which tunes can be played.

Drums and Other Un-tuned Percussion

What do you do if your child – at any age from six to sixteen – comes to you and pesters week after week with: 'I want to play the drums'? Every group on television, most of the music on radio, whatever he sees and hears, seems to reinforce his interest in the drums and his desire to play them.

In the case of the six-year-old, of course, he *may* just be telling you that he wants to play something. Six-year-olds often pick the drum as their fantasy instrument because it is the easiest one for them to hear: it does not trick their ears by changing pitch like the melodic instruments.

The same child at eight, when he is ready to learn, will have an ear which can identify and appreciate melodic sounds. But the child old enough to begin, and who wants to play the drums, leaves you in no doubt about his suitability. He is probably a hyperactive child – one who is still wide awake at midnight or who rises three hours before the rest of the family.

Any parent with such a child is well-advised to spend time on this section of the book, for taking up percussion seriously has been the salvation of many a hyperactive child.

Learning percussion properly does not mean filling the bedroom with drums large and small and destroying everyone's peace with the thump of bass-drum night and day. A proper course of study begins with just the side-drum. A non-drummer rarely understands that a child can happily learn the side-drum for years before needing to go on to other instruments. Indeed, an orchestral percussionist may spend twenty years perfecting his side-drum roll – and still feel that he never played it perfectly!

The side-drum requires regular lessons from a teacher, whether the eventual ambition is to appear on the platform of the Royal Festival Hall in the percussion section of an orchestra, or on the scaffolding at a rock festival. Practising between lessons at home can be done with a practice pad over the drum to muffle the sound. Many young drummers are banished to the garage or garden shed, but it doesn't seem to bother them a tenth as much as not being able to practice.

After acquiring a basic technique on the side-drum, the young drummer can move in two directions. If, at thirteen or fourteen, he is beginning to get 'into the rock scene', his side-drum technique gives him a head start for taking up the drumkit.

If he or she is attracted to classical music, or the idea of playing in an orchestra, the young drummer moves on, under the percussion teacher, to learn about the other un-tuned percussion instruments. Each one has its own technique and demands slightly different skills.

In one piece of music the orchestral percussionist may change from playing side-drum to cymbals to wood-block to gong to maracas to bass-drum. What better therapy for the unbearable fidget than to find that his or her natural tendency to drop one thing and immediately pick up an-other is no longer regarded as a nuisance, but as ideal musical behaviour? (Out of the whole orchestra, only the percussionists stand, move about and constantly change instruments during the music.)

Physical Suitability

The child who truly wants to play the drums does more than just talk about it. He drums – with or without music – using his fingers, hands, sticks, knives and forks, on tables, chairs and any surface that comes to hand. He is a real 'fidget', who is constantly discharging nervous tension with repetitive small movements.

Drummers are thin, wiry. They often have a huge appetite but never seem to put on weight. They have more stamina than larger, apparently stronger children.

Mental Suitability

Bright, quick-witted children, who have a natural tendency towards the 'butterfly' attitude of starting something and then moving on to the next activity, find a therapy and outlet for their mental energy in percussion. Classroom teachers and parents are often amazed how the child who never settled to anything else can become absorbed in learning percussion technique – practising conscientiously for hours every week over a period of years. What sounds to the untrained ear like two hours of the same beat, is, to a drummer's discriminating ear, a series of subtle variations – what they call, onomatopoeiacally, 'paradiddles'.

Personality Suitability

Tense, nervous, often irritable, hyperactive, restless: some of these characteristics are typical of the potential drummer, who is often considerably more independent of the family than other children of the same age.

SUITABILITY SUMMARY	✓ OR ✗
Physical	
Mental	
Personality	

Drumkit

Few children younger than thirteen have the extraordinary co-ordination necessary even to begin playing the drumkit. The kit-player may be doing one thing with his right hand, something quite different with his left – and each foot may simultaneously have its own pattern of activity!

The best preparation for a younger child who really wants to learn the kit is to spend a year or two acquiring side-drum technique. He is then far more likely to succeed on the kit than a child who starts by trying to play simultaneously all the instruments of the kit.

Because many adolescent drummers have prepared themselves badly (if at all), the young drummer who has had lessons on side-drum and percussion technique finds himself welcome not just in rock groups, but also in jazz groups, dance bands, big bands, brass bands – nowadays even occasionally in full youth orchestras when the repertoire includes modern pieces.

A kit-player who can read music and has had basic training can find opportunities to play any kind of music he enjoys.

SUITABILITY SUMMARY	✓ OR ✗
General	

Tuned Percussion and Timpani

The tuned percussion include xylophone, chime bars, glockenspiel, also vibraphone and marimba. All these instruments are based on the same logic as the piano keyboard.

Virtually all children who take up these instruments seriously are either pianists who have been learning for several years and are bored or want to be able to join an orchestra or band, or are un-tuned percussionists who are required to learn these instruments to play in youth orchestras. Almost never is a serious course of study on these instruments the direct result of playing in junior-school percussion bands. To play tuned percussion properly requires a degree of dexterity and co-ordination extremely rare in children under twelve or thirteen.

The timpani are tuneable drums. Tuning them whilst playing is highly skilled. Drummers with an acute sense of pitch are recommended to transfer to the timps by conductors of school or youth orchestras. These are not first instruments. Virtually no children will succeed on these instruments without prior musical training.

More important than specific physical, mental and personality characteristics are:

• a strong desire to play in band or orchestra;

- a thorough basic training on either piano or un-tuned percussion or any other orchestral instrument;
- above-average dexterity.

SUITABILITY SUMMARY	✓ OR ✗
General	

THINKING ABOUT THE SELF-CONTAINED INSTRUMENTS

All the instruments so far considered belong to orchestras or bands, in one or other of the four main suits of instruments: woodwind, brass, strings and percussion. Because they are *designed* for group music-making, few of them offer much to the truly solitary child. Only the flute, violin, French horn and perhaps the cello offer long-term satisfaction to the child who wants to be and play alone.

The jokers in our pack are for solitary children. The piano, guitar and harp are self-contained instruments each of which can play either single notes or chords. Thus, they can play tunes but they can also provide their own harmonies. (To a limited extent this is also true of the tuned percussion.)

These instruments are difficult. Learning one of them demands far more of a child mentally than learning a woodwind or brass instrument but offers in return one distinct reward: from a very early stage, you can play a complete (albeit simple) piece of music, needing no other players for harmony or musical completeness.

The question most often asked by parents is: when is *the right age* to start piano/guitar/harp lessons?

The right age to start is between eight and ten, when the kind of child suited to the self-contained instruments becomes bored at school. Of above-average intelligence, they are among the earliest to be literate and numerate. For them, the first couple of years at school are exciting, but by the third year in primary school they are expected – unless in an exceptional school – to mark time while the less able catch them up.

What happens? These children become bored and lazy. They lose the ability to concentrate and their standards of achievement steadily decline, often to the mystification of teachers and parents alike. The remedy is to give these children something to expand the mentality, the intelligence and the imagination. Learning to play one of the self-contained instruments can do all this.

Piano

For many music-lovers, a Mozart piano concerto is the epitome of musical beauty. For many young children, the piano itself is a medieval torture-machine. More people have been musically crippled by the piano than by all the other instruments put together.

If that seems a startling statement, ask a few adult friends who had piano lessons (a) how much they enjoyed them, (b) do they still play, (c) did they ever learn to read music fluently, (d) can they still read music . . . and (e) (the crunch question) did it really enrich their lives?

So many people have come to us for counselling about the piano that for years we were baffled why such a large number of potentially musical, often highly intelligent children and adults had been traumatized to the point of not being able to read a note of music – all by their early experiences on the piano. After analysing hundreds of cases, we found that the majority started lessons between five and seven. This is one of the most stressful periods of a lifetime. The child is busy enough trying to come to terms with school, other children, having to absorb abstract knowledge, become literate and numerate and so on. The last thing he or she needs is an additional mental burden during that crucial period.

By far the majority of children put on to the piano at this stressful period build up a mental block about musical notation, about learning an instrument, about their own musical potential. This is a block which can and often does last for life.

So, what kind of child does succeed on the piano?

Physical Suitability

Because the piano is a machine which does most of the physical work of producing the sound, it can be played equally well by the frail or the strong. It does not demand physical energy, but rather the reverse: the ability to be comfortable and at ease seated on the piano stool for half an hour or more at a time. Physically energetic children dislike this. Delicate children who are happy to do this enjoy the power of the sound they can produce on the piano.

Children with less than normal vision find it a considerable strain to read double-clef music and, simultaneously, check visually the changing position of hands and fingers (on no other commonly learnt instrument do the player's hand and finger positions change from the very beginning). Statistically, children with below-average eyesight are less likely to succeed on the piano than those of equal musical potential with good eyesight.

Playing advanced piano music requires precise and complicated co-ordination of all ten digits. However, progress on the instrument is so slow that the pupil develops precise digital control by the time it is required. Children who have learnt the piano for several years make rapid and accurate typists, mechanics, machinists, surgeons. They excel at any activity which requires both hands and several fingers to be used at the same time.

It is sometimes said that a child must be able to span an

octave before starting to learn. This is usually an indirect way of saying that the child is too young. In fact, a span of five notes is quite sufficient to start with. Because the piano is a machine which does the work for you, most children of average physique from five upwards could fulfil the physical requirement sufficiently to begin learning.

Mental Suitability

The mental requirements are the problem. Few children under the age of seven can satisfy them; few children under the age of seven can appreciate the rewards, either.

A child who is still working hard at reading and/or writing and/or arithmetic, or is experiencing the social pressures of school simply does not have the spare mental energy to come to terms with double-clef notation and all those keys! Such a child only makes apparent progress if 'pushed' or helped by a parent at daily practice sessions. Essentially this progress lasts as long as the parent's spare energy. Single children and youngest-in-the-family can be taught the piano in this way, because they have a parent who can supply the mental energy which the child lacks.

Reading and playing piano music requires a brain good at mental arithmetic. To such a mentality it is pleasurable to read and decipher two notational codes simultaneously and translate this information into precise finger positions – at the rate of ten or twenty 'dots' per second – with different rhythms – with varying pressure – with feet co-ordinated – with intelligence of expression, etc., etc.!

To summarize mental suitability for this complicated instrument, the child with a reasonable chance of success on the piano will be:

- at or near the top of the class

- seven or older, with spare mental energy after all the demands of school have been met
- good at mental arithmetic
- naturally conscientious and painstaking
- possibly beginning to get lazy, waiting for 'the others to catch up' at school.

Except for the very, very rare prodigies, progress on the piano is achieved by the steady application of intelligence over a long period.

Personality Suitability

A quietly intelligent and conscientious child is rewarded by a slow but sure series of achievements where each advance of technique opens new avenues of musical pleasure. At every stage of learning, there is an infinity of music written for the piano – in every possible style from classical to the latest rock.

Gregarious children are miserable on the piano, for it takes many years of study before this instrument can be played with others. Sometimes, however, they transfer to an orchestral or band or group instrument after learning piano for a couple of years. The piano provides an unrivalled basis of musicianship, so these children usually do very well on their second instrument.

The true pianist is a natural loner who likes privacy – perhaps a refuge from the hustle and bustle of older siblings. He or she may be shy or an exhibitionist, but either way is not the kind to 'join in' or want to be part of a group. He or she has an instinctive desire to be self-sufficient.

An only child – or one with very much older brothers and sisters – is used to relating to adults. Such a child is more likely to enjoy and profit from the strong and prolonged teacher/pupil relationship than a child who is happier with other children and does not relate easily to adults.

Some children who are – or feel that they are – 'small for their age' get deep satisfaction, and therefore motivation, from the sound they can make on such a powerful instrument. It may be an aspect of this phenomenon that attracts so many young children to the piano, when they are still far too young to begin learning properly.

The piano is too little exploited as a second instrument for older children. Many children begin learning a single-note instrument, but find eventually that the technique is insufficiently demanding or the music unstimulating for them. If they are naturally self-contained and have the right mentality, their two or three years' learning on the first instrument enables them to make such good progress on the piano that, in some cases, they overtake co-evals who began on the piano much earlier. 'Late developers' can find this the best route to the piano.

Older children whose creativity expresses itself in a desire to compose music will be fascinated by the logic of the keyboard and the harmonic possibilities of the piano.

SUITABILITY SUMMARY	✓ OR ✗
Physical	
Mental	
Personality	

Classical Guitar

The classical guitar is an instrument as serious as any in this book. It can be many things to many different children and almost needs a book of its own to explain what it can offer to your child and which kind of children can benefit from it.

There is much to commend it:

- the guitar is a progressive instrument. Its rewards and satisfactions for the right child are equal to those offered by piano or violin. It is as difficult and demanding technically as either of those instruments and therefore pursuing a course of study on the guitar can contribute as much to the child's personal development as learning either of them;
- the guitar has one major advantage for children over piano and violin in that those are the instruments of yesterday, while the guitar is the instrument of tomorrow;
- at any level of learning, there is an endless level of repertoire to play and enjoy;
- it is a quiet instrument delightful to hear coming from the bedroom even on the first fumbling attempts of the youngest beginner – the very first scales sound musical;
- after the initial stages, relatively little parental support is

called for, although it is always an excellent idea for parents to listen from time to time to the pieces being worked on, even if the child resists this;

- learning the guitar confers peer-group approval, so important for the child lacking in self-confidence. Few children are ashamed of learning the guitar or give it up because of hostile pressure from school-mates. Boys who live in areas of large cities where they 'would not be seen dead' carrying a violin case find no stigma attached to walking to the weekly lessons carrying a guitar case – thanks to the Beatles and their successors;

- like the piano, it is a self-contained instrument with no need for others to play with and so has a lot to offer the child who through illness, geography or lack of inclination cannot or will not go out and find group music-making opportunities;

- because reading and playing the music is mentally very absorbing but not too demanding physically, the daily practice can be an excellent therapy for asthmatic and other delicate children who need their minds taken off their physical condition;

- an instrument for the beginner is cheap, less than half the cost of an equivalent-quality flute, or a fraction of the cost of a piano;

- unlike the strings or brass, it requires little sense of pitch.

Why then do so many children give up learning the guitar? Anyone reading this book will know that some fail because they are not suited to the instrument, but in the case of the guitar, there is another equally important reason: children and parents alike are hoodwinked by the media into thinking that the guitar is an easy instrument to play and that quick results can be achieved with little or no effort.

Nothing could be further from the truth. It takes two or three years of weekly lessons, daily practice and conscientious application to reach the level of playing graded pieces. Luckily many modern children are highly attracted to the guitar and motivated to work much harder at it than they would at any of the orchestral instruments or the piano. However, rarely does a child progress on the guitar without first making a conscious decision to work. The technique of the instrument is difficult, and so also is the music.

Physical Suitability

Playing the classical guitar (as distinct from folk or electric guitar) uses seven fingers and the right thumb. It develops a quite outstanding degree of digital co-ordination. Children who are good with their fingers – model-builders, girls who like needlework – make a good start.

The player must 'stop' up to six strings at a time, using all four fingers of the left hand and simultaneously co-ordinate three fingers and the thumb of the right hand to pluck the correct string or strings with a particular finger or fingers: a degree of physical and mental co-ordination at least as high as that called for when playing the piano with both hands.

Playing the guitar correctly *develops* considerable strength in the fingers, wrists and forearms and for this reason it is often taken up by children who are not robust. The fingers of the left hand must be trained to cope with considerable stretches but the beginner, particularly the younger child starting on a small-size instrument, develops this technique gradually.

To make the playing position as comfortable as possible and avoid bad playing habits which will eventually result in giving up learning, it is important to ensure that children start on a guitar which is not too large. There are three-quarter and half-size guitars to suit children who are physically too small for a full-size instrument.

Mental Suitability

Whilst young children can be physically comfortable on the small-size guitars, few are mentally ready for the hard work of learning before eight or nine, when the pressure at school is relaxed for a couple of years.

The best progress is made by children who are good at mental arithmetic and good with their hands.

The *genuine* slow learner (the child who cannot absorb abstract concepts and cannot retain information), or the child whose co-ordination is poor will not be happy on this instrument. However, sometimes the label 'slow learner' is loosely applied to a child who is unhappy in a competitive classroom situation, yet naturally methodical and conscientious in hobbies, for example. Such a child can do far better on the guitar than any school record would suggest. Indeed, many outstanding guitar pupils have poor school reports.

Personality Suitability

The sound is produced by a repeated plucking motion from the fingers of the right hand. This movement, and the method of holding the guitar close, right in front of the body, seems to be deeply comforting and pleasurable to the acquisitive or possessive child – perhaps a collector, or a hoarder of pocket money.

Chess-players feel good reading and playing guitar music. There is something about the classical guitar and its music (far from the image of flamenco and gypsies, etc.) that satisfies the unemotional child, the child who does not want open or equal-sided relationships. Unlike piano children, who enjoy relating to adults, the guitar-learner is typically self-contained and independent. It is almost a requirement that he should be, because unless a parent or older sibling also plays the guitar, there is no one to whom he can talk about the problems and pleasures of learning and playing this instrument. The weekly visit to the guitar teacher is just about the only time in the week when the child can 'open up'.

The child who succeeds on the guitar enjoys being alone, wants to be independent and will work hard and determinedly to achieve independence. There are few opportunities for group music-making on the classical guitar.

SUITABILITY SUMMARY	✓ OR ✗
Physical	
Mental	
Personality	

Harp

If many parents overlook the guitar, few indeed will ever think of the harp. How many modern homes even have space for an instrument five feet high and four feet wide? How many children want to pluck 46 strings using two thumbs and eight fingers and operate seven pedals using both feet? As if that's not enough, the 46 strings all have to be tuned – by the player!

Well, some children hear a harp or see it on television perhaps for the first time and just *know* this heavenly instrument is for them.

No child is ever in two minds about learning the harp. It is not a candidate for many Short Lists. The would-be harp-player will tell Mum and Dad again and again and again that this is the one instrument which he or she wants to play. What do you do about it? You cannot just walk into the local music shop and buy one. Even when you have found a harp, it will have a price ticket to make you gasp: several hundred pounds for an old one which needs attention and several thousand for a good new one.

What do you do if it is going to be two or three years before your child can have one? The best preparation meanwhile is to learn the piano. While not physically satisfying, this familiarizes the child with treble- and bass-clef notation, as read by a harpist.

Most harp children begin – especially in Wales – on the smaller, cheaper and easier-to-play Celtic harp which has only 29 strings, is easily portable and has no pedals to bother a beginner. Only very self-contained, shy children, mainly girls, will want to spend many hours a week practising either Celtic or orchestral harp. No parent can help much except by providing occasional transport (for lessons, you use the teacher's harp or, in Wales, the school instrument). An orchestral harp takes two adults to manoeuvre into one of the larger estate cars.

What are the rewards? Solo harp music is transcendently beautiful to play and listen to; the harp is a wonderful instrument to accompany the human voice – either the player's or a friend's; and, if you have transport, any youth orchestra for older children will welcome a harpist.

It is difficult to find anyone to give advice about the harp, for few schoolteachers or even professional musicians know anything about it, so, if your child passionately wants to play it, write to your nearest professional orchestra and ask the harpist to give you and your child some advice before or after a rehearsal. Do not expect written advice. You will have to be prepared to travel and be there when it suits the harpist's busy schedule, but it is the only way. Harpists are fanatical about their instrument as well as being extremely helpful people. Few of them will turn down a polite and reasonable request for help – after all, they know the problems you have.

SUITABILITY SUMMARY	✓ OR ✗
General	

THINKING ABOUT THE
SELF-TAUGHT INSTRUMENTS

All the instruments so far examined have one thing in common: they are learnt formally. Children study them by following a progressive course of structured lessons under the tuition of trained teachers, with progress measured by regular examinations. The child knows how well he or she is doing. A succession of achievements in graded exams builds the child's confidence. The child is able to understand the relationship between work and results, which leads to an early development of self-discipline. Learning an instrument in this way contributes much to the child's developing character.

There are no such advantages for children on the self-taught instruments. They are learnt informally: by ear, by trial and error, by painstakingly copying the sounds heard on cassettes and records. It is rarely possible to find lessons. When tuition is available, it is usually given by an older amateur player, not a trained teacher, who may – or may not – have evolved his own pattern of learning the instrument. Most players cannot read music.

Whilst few children can succeed in learning an instrument in this manner, many adolescents need to be free from adult teachers. They want to achieve something by their own efforts and with some help from friends. They want informality and independence and are prepared to devote great energy to what is, comparatively, a far more difficult way of learning an instrument.

Electric Guitar

All electric instruments – guitar, bass and keyboards – are designed to make a lot of noise. They can be played quietly, but what sounds quiet to the player can be intolerably loud to the other occupants of the house. Most of the music they play – and this is the reason why adolescents want them – is as aggressive as a motorbike. The problem even for the young player who has promised to practise quietly is similar to that of the motorcyclist who has undertaken not to exceed 15 m.p.h. – it is too unsatisfying.

This instrument is not hollow like the classical guitar. It is solid and heavy to hold and play. The weight burden and the stretches required of the left hand make it uncomfortable for most children until about thirteen, although younger children *determined* to play it will put up with a great deal of discomfort, such is the appeal of these instruments. The fingertips of the left hand can become very sore from pressing against the steel strings.

Junk shops are full of guitars abandoned by once-hopeful children who were too young to start or who thought it was all going to be so easy. The player must practise for many hours a week to acquire the co-ordination of right and left hands. The music is rarely written and proper teaching is almost impossible to find. Teaching yourself to play even a few chords by ear is hard.

The musical miracle of these instruments is not that so many give up, but rather that so many persevere on their own to the stage where they can begin playing with friends. It is a pity that the school system has little interest in, or way of recognizing, this hard work, and does little to help.

That all sounds so negative, but before you heave a sigh of relief that all your worst fears and prejudices have been confirmed, let us ponder what good these instruments do, what they have to offer your child in terms of personal development. Surprisingly, quite a lot.

Most adolescent boys need to get away from parents, teachers, siblings and even girls of their own age. They need a valid reason to get together with other young males in self-organized groups doing something masculine. Playing an electric instrument or the drumkit in a group does all this *and* it confers status in the eyes of school-mates. If you and the family can somehow cope with the noise problem, this hobby can make a teenage son *easier* to live with, giving him always 'something to do', the physical pleasure of playing a powerful instrument, a development of nervous and muscular co-ordination, the satisfaction of making musical progress, a sense of achievement which builds identity, an ever-present relief from the tensions of adolescence and a wonderful way of making new friendships.

If a child younger than eleven or twelve insists that he wants to play the electric guitar, what does a parent do?

Well, it must be borne in mind that these instruments contain live mains voltage, which can kill. The player inevitably takes guitar and amp to pieces, changes parts, cures problems. This is obviously dangerous if the child is too young to understand electricity. Also, the instrument and its necessary amplifier cost more than many parents are pre-pared to spend.

We suggest in these circumstances that the child be encouraged to start saving pocket money towards the cost of instrument and amplifier, whilst, at the same time, beginning lessons on either a single-note instrument or the classical guitar – as a preparation for the electric guitar.

SUITABILITY SUMMARY	✓ OR ✗
General	

Bass Guitar

Every teenage rock group needs a good bass-player. Many school bands, brass bands, big bands and dance bands use a bass guitar instead of the old-fashioned (and often inaudible) double bass. Any teenager who has learnt to read bass clef on piano, cello, double bass or bassoon can pick up a bass guitar and within a couple of weeks be launched on an exciting new hobby. The electric guitar requires chordal technique; the bass plays only one note at a time. What music exists is easy to read and play.

Like all the other bass instruments, the bass guitar is frustrating for the aggressive extrovert. For a tall, responsive adolescent who does not want to hog the limelight yet wishes to have a ready passport to rock group or band, it is a wonderful Christmas or birthday present.

SUITABILITY SUMMARY	✓ OR ✗
General	

Electric Keyboards

Music shops have a bewildering range of electric keyboards. They fall into four groups:

- small portable keyboards;
- electric pianos which reproduce the sound of a mechanical piano;
- electronic organs with two manuals and foot pedals;
- synthesizers and workstations.

Small portable keyboards are often bought as educational toys for children. With their in-built rhythms and instrument-mimicking range of sounds they make the first encounter with the keyboard fun. Many come with free teach-yourself methods which enable a small repertoire of tunes to be picked out, but few young children can teach themselves beyond this level. To be used as a serious learning instrument, a keyboard must be 'touch-sensitive', have a range of at least four octaves and keys of conventional piano width (many are narrower). Piano exams up to Grade 5 may be taken on such an instrument.

Some people do not agree with manufacturers' claims that **electronic pianos** sound the same as traditional instruments, but they do have important advantages: they stay in tune (which avoids the expense of twice-yearly visits from the tuner), they take up less space in the home and are reasonably portable from room to room and house to house. Flat-dwellers may find them useful because they can be played silently, using headphones. Many children are more attracted to the modern image of these instruments than to the old-fashioned upright piano. For an older child it is important to buy one with a midi port.

Electronic organs are rarely first instruments but may appeal to the child who has been learning piano and wants another self-contained instrument on which to become more creative or adventurous with sound, exploiting the in-built rhythms and effects. Like the other electric keyboards, organs can be played using headphones, without disturbing either neighbours or the rest of the family.

Synthesizers and workstations are not learning instruments. Often bought as bribes to continue piano lessons, they are essentially machines on which a musically creative adolescent can experiment with sound, improvise and compose, limited only by his or her own creativity. Many players are self-taught but, because the design is based on the logic of the piano keyboard, an adolescent who has learnt piano will get off to a flying start on a synthesizer. Like the first payment to the Mafia, buying a synthesizer can be expensive, not just for itself but because the list of ancillary equipment – midi interfaces, sequencers, memories, rhythm boxes, recording equipment and music computers – is endless!

SUITABILITY SUMMARY	✓ OR ✗
General	

Folk Guitar

Some teenagers are naturally quiet individuals. Not for them the aggressive atmosphere of a rock group, nor the unavoidable sociability of a folk club. Yet, between fifteen and twenty, they begin to feel that they have missed out on music by not having proper lessons on an instrument during childhood, or by having given them up.

The folk guitar, played solo or accompanying their own or a friend's voice, can be the answer. This is a light, hollow-bodied acoustic instrument. It looks like a large classical guitar, but the strings are made of steel, to give a louder, harsher sound.

It takes a reasonably good ear to progress beyond the level of a few basic chords and a good musical instinct to improvise harmonic accompaniments – about the same as shown by Grandad when he used to bang out 'songs from the shows' on the drawing-room piano. The capo is a device clamped on to the strings to make playing easier. Lessons are rarely obtainable, but, because the instrument is widely self-taught by people of all ages, there are many excellent tutor-books on the market.

Some junior schools offer folk guitar group lessons, in which the children learn a few basic chords and to pick out a small repertoire of tunes. This is nothing like studying classical guitar technique. However, a child who enjoys these group lessons, who wants to learn the guitar properly and who satisfies the three-way suitability criteria, has a good motivation to begin learning classical guitar.

SUITABILITY SUMMARY	✓ OR ✗
General	

Traditional and Folk Instruments

Traditional and folk instruments can be great fun for sociable children and adolescents. These include folk fiddles, acoustic and electric guitars, string and electric bass, dulcimers, lutes, drums, tambourines, recorders, Celtic harps, accordions (both piano and button), whistles, steel drums, pipes and many traditional instruments such as the bagpipes. Played in schools and youth clubs their positive media image attracts many children who would not be drawn to formal music-making. Most of these instruments are learnt by ear and usually played without written music. Enthusiasm is the common characteristic of conductors and organizers, which is why youth workers encourage children who would never go near a youth orchestra to get involved in this kind of activity. Within the framework of 'creative music-making' in schools, children are encouraged to make their own music on these instruments which produce sounds more exciting to the untrained ear than the conventional orchestral instruments.

SUITABILITY SUMMARY	✓ OR ✗
General	

Other Fretted Instruments

Because so few children hear or see fretted instruments being played, they do not commonly figure on lists of 'Instruments I Would Like To Play'. (Frets are the thin bars fixed across the neck of guitars, banjoes, mandolins and other plucked and strummed instruments.)

This group of instruments includes:

- banjoes, ukeleles;
- mandolins, lutes;
- various regional and national plucked and strummed instruments; for instance, the balalaika.

These instruments had a great vogue of popularity before skiffle and electric instruments ousted them from fashion.

Yet some children hear these instruments for the first time and are instantly attracted by the sound. They 'just know' that the mandolin, or the . . . is the instrument they have been looking for. Mostly, the fretted instruments appeal to older children who like the 'atmosphere' of a banjo band, a ukelele orchestra or a lute group, without quite knowing why.

What kind of children are they?

They are generally quiet in behaviour and voice.

Introspective but not withdrawn. Intelligent, but not sharp or bright. 'Good with their fingers.' Patient and conscientious. Subject to enthusiasms, sometimes collectors.

These instruments are satisfying to practise and play at home, because both melodies and chords can be played on them. They are not noisy, which can be a great advantage in thin-walled modern accommodation. Played in groups, they have the quiet intensity of a chamber orchestra.

Because most of the music is specially arranged for the ensemble, the repertoire is as wide as the players want it to be. The clubs and bands are organized by devoted amateurs. Help in finding instruments, guidance and some kind of lessons can usually be obtained through the club or band.

Except for the largest bass instruments, all the fretted instruments are comfortable to hold and play.

A few solitary adolescents take up mandolin or lute as a solo instrument, learning to play by ear only. To play in any kind of group, however, necessitates learning to read music. As in the brass band, this does not seem to be a problem for the well-motivated. They 'pick it up as they go along'.

SUITABILITY SUMMARY	✓ OR ✗
General	

Stage Three

Finalizing the Choice

Your child's Short List is now made up of the small number of instruments which have no cross on their Suitability Summary. One of them is the Right Instrument. So close, and yet so far? Not at all – getting rid of the others until only the Right One is left is the easiest stage of the whole process. In fact, your child does most of the work, as you will see.

The majority of children's Short Lists have only two or three instruments. Reducing them to the Right Instrument is done with the child. However, it is possible that you have five or more instruments which have no crosses against them. If so, you have an intermediate stage to carry out, before involving the child.

Reducing the Short List – without the child

Eliminate the marginal instruments in the following order:

1. The instruments which sound least like your child's voice. (This may seem a strange idea when you first read the words, but it makes sense. Children are

naturally and instinctively attracted to those instruments which sound approximately in the same register as their own voices. This explains why so many children are drawn to the treble instruments such as flute, recorder, clarinet, cornet, violin. Many young children find it hard to hear bass, or low-sounding, instruments and no child can be highly motivated to learn an instrument which is hard for the player to hear.)

2. Instruments which would be too expensive to buy or hire. (Bassoon or harp, for example, are outside most family budgets.)

3. Instruments too large to have in the home or to transport. (Piano, tuba, double bass, harp may simply be too cumbersome for many modern houses and flats.)

4. Instruments (other than self-taught) for which there are no lessons available locally. (Your music shop or public library can give you information.)

By the time you have eliminated these four categories of marginal instruments, the Short List should be manageable. The next stage is done by you and the child together.

The Short List

Tick only those instruments which have no crosses on their Suitability Summary.

WOODWIND	✓
Flute	
Clarinet	
Saxophone	
Oboe	
Bassoon	
Recorder	

BRASS	✓
Cornet	
Trumpet	
Tenor Horn/Baritone	
Trombone	
Euphonium	
Tuba/E Flat/B Flat Bass	
French Horn	

STRINGS	✓
Violin	
Viola	
Cello	
Double Bass	

PERCUSSION	✓
Drums/Un-tuned Percussion Drumkit Tuned Percussion/Timpani	
SELF-CONTAINED INSTRUMENTS	✓
Piano Classical Guitar Harp	
SELF-TAUGHT INSTRUMENTS	✓
Electric Guitar Bass Guitar Electric Keyboards/Organs Folk Guitar Traditional and Folk Instruments Fretted Instruments	

Reducing the Short List — with the child

You and your child go to the largest, or the most friendly, music shop in the area and try all the instruments on the Short List. It's as simple as that.

The staff will help, by showing your child how to assemble the instruments properly, how to hold them and how to produce a note. If the child is shy, they can usually find a private cubicle or studio at the back of the shop where he or she can try the instruments without embarrassment or distraction.

The child will tell you which one feels nice and which does not; which is too heavy or too large to hold, or demands too much energy to play; which 'makes a nice sound' – in short, which is the Right One.

The parent's only problem is that, having done so much hard work to get to this stage, it is tempting to interfere when the child is trying the instruments. Be content with a background role. You are there just to deal with the assistants in the shop. Your child is in charge of the selection itself.

At our Music Centre, we frequently had a hundred or more children trying their Short List instruments on a single day. Almost all of them just knew that they did or did not like the violin/cornet/flute by the simple expedient of holding it (under guidance) and producing a few notes on it.

Some children may be luke-warm about one or two instruments, but all children can quickly say which instruments they either like or do not like – provided the parent does not make suggestions. It can be difficult to avoid 'loaded' questions like: 'That's a lovely violin. Did you like it?' To this sort of question, most children try to give the answer they think the parent wants.

Buying a musical instrument is – at any age – a very personal matter. Let the child take as much time as he or she wishes. Don't restrict the try-outs to one go on each instrument. Your child – as the potential owner of a real musical instrument – deserves VIP treatment in any music shop. You will find that the staff understand the problems. They would far rather sell you the Right Instrument after three or four visits than a wrong one on the first day you go into the shop.

A musical instrument is not just another toy. The Right Instrument may be the most important possession you ever buy for your child.

Parental Follow-Up

Parental Follow-Up

Ahead of you and your child now lie many magical, shared moments, ranging from the first experimental notes and simple tunes to 'real music', examination successes, joining an orchestra or band, playing at festivals and public concerts. A lifetime enriched by the ability to make music stretches before your child.

Yet, during the years of learning, there are moments when every parent needs some guidance. The notes in these last pages answer the most frequent pleas for help received from parents who had used the earlier editions of *The Right Instrument for your Child*.

Buying or Borrowing an Instrument

To buy or to borrow? That is the question.

Children do not grow out of instruments as quickly as they do their shoes or bicycles. Most professional wood-wind and brass musicians have had only three or four instruments in their lives. For example, I began learning on a Selmer Gold Seal flute, up-graded to a Yamaha student flute and then moved on to my professional flute, a Rudall Carte wooden flute made in 1903 as an apprentice piece. I now play an Althus silver flute with an Oxley gold head-joint because it travels better and copes with climate changes.

Because replacing an instrument is not an annual expenditure, for woodwind and brass it is worth buying what the music shop calls 'a good beginner instrument' and upgrading to a better model after Grade 5. After Grade 8, the learner needs a semi-pro or student instrument.

The stringed instruments can be found in half or quarter sizes. The young learner does grow out of these, but since they have few moving parts, good ones lose little or no value when it comes to trading them in for a bigger size. Once on the full-size stringed instruments, the rule is to buy the best you can afford.

How much should one pay for a good beginner instrument? Professional musicians spend hundreds, even thousands, of pounds on their instruments, but the 'student' instruments on which children begin to learn cost far less. They are priced by the manufacturers to be within range of the average family budget. It is worthwhile to visit several music shops, since they do not all have the same range of instruments on offer. Shop around; prices vary.

Because the international musical instrument market is very competitive, prices are a guide to quality. In general, the more you pay, the better the instrument. The very cheapest instruments may have defects which will handicap the learner, or at least cause disappointment. If subsequently you wish to sell the instrument or to trade it in for a better one, the additional investment to buy a better instrument in the first place will more than be justified. Unlike toys or domestic appliances, proper musical instruments hold their value well, the better ones even appreciating as time goes by. Electric instruments, on the other hand, lose value overnight – like a new car. When buying outright, it is quite usual to ask for, and be given, one week's approval, in order to have the instrument vetted by the teacher.

Many parents prefer not to buy outright. Any reputable music shop will offer two other possibilities. Hire purchase is as normal for instruments as for refrigerators and television sets. Peculiar to music is the hire-and-buy system, whereby you hire the instrument from the shop for a trial period and the hire fee is deducted from the purchase price if you eventually decide to buy. The advantages are obvious. Of the three ways to obtain a new instrument, this is the one we recommend.

Most music shops also have a selection of used instruments. The prices may not be lower than for new models, but you should get better value for money – in other words, a better quality instrument – when buying a guaranteed second-hand instrument.

Buying privately is a more risky business. Most local papers carry advertisements for private sale of used instruments and local junk shops often have musical instruments displayed in the window. If you do find what seems to be a bargain in either of these ways, it is worth paying a small fee to your local music shop, or a teacher or musician, to examine the instrument before purchase is completed. Many defects are not obvious to the layman, nor even to players of other instruments, yet can be a crippling disadvantage to the child beginner.

It is in some areas possible to borrow an instrument long-term through the school system. This can be a good idea, in order to get started before funds are available for purchase. However, such loaned instruments have often been damaged or neglected by a previous borrower. They should always be thoroughly overhauled by a trained repairer before the child begins to learn.

Lastly, brass bands normally lend instruments long-term to any child who joins the junior section.

Buying an Instrument on the Internet

If there are hazards in buying second-hand through a news-paper advertisement, there are a thousand times more via the Internet. The established auction and exchange sites like eBay warn users of perils such as losing their money and getting nothing for it, or divulging credit-card information, etc. In the case of a musical instrument, there are all the normal risks *plus* the likelihood that there may be something wrong with the instrument, such as a badly effected repair that goes wrong after a few days or weeks.

Electronic instruments may have defective transistors that are expensive to replace or are irreplaceable. Even in good condition, once superseded by newer models they are often worthless anyway.

On brass instruments, there can be problems of sticking valves which are impossible to cure; a trombone may have an invisible bend in the slide that makes it impossible to play properly.

A stringed instrument may have worn pegs that will not 'lock' and therefore make tuning a nightmare. The bodies are delicate and may have been damaged and repaired; if professionally done, this does not matter, but a DIY repair may spell disaster. Or perhaps the fiddle or cello is OK but the bow needs re-hairing or is warped and cannot be re-haired. That may cost you far more than you are saving. And if there's a yellow maker's label inside bearing the name Cremona? It's highly unlikely to be a genuine Strad . . .

The general rule is that the more moving parts, the

smaller the chance of buying an unseen instrument with good results. On woodwind instruments, keys that seem to work alright might not close perfectly; pads may need replacing, which is expensive; rods and springs may be impossible to adjust correctly; dry solder joints may snap after little use. On saxes, the octave key may be defective. Instruments made of wood (many are now plastic) may have longitudinal cracks concealed by shellac that open up after a short time.

Brass and woodwind instruments might simply be old and 'played out'. Although polished and cleaned to look like new to the uninitiated, they will never make a decent sound.

So, if thinking about buying via the Internet, beware, beware and beware! The risk is not just financial: a child trying to learn on a defective instrument becomes demoralized and loses the impetus of that initial excitement with long-term negative effect.

If you still feel that you have found a bargain on the Internet, insist on having it for a week's approval before parting with your cash and take it to a reputable music shop for examination. The fee you pay for this service may save you a lot of money.

Finding a Teacher

Depending where you live, it can be easy or difficult to find a teacher for a particular instrument. Teachers of the 'traditional' instruments like piano and violin are more widely available than their colleagues who specialize in giving, say, French horn or saxophone tuition. Many music teachers belong to The Incorporated Society of Musicians, at 10 Stratford Place, London W1C 1AA (Tel: 0207 629 4413).

Your local library should have a list of music teachers in

the area. *Yellow Pages* list both music schools and individual teachers. Local music shops usually keep a list of teachers and, in many cases, have studios on the premises where lessons are given.

Some school systems offer instrumental lessons either privately or in groups. Normally, these lessons are restricted to those instruments for which teachers happen to be available within the system.

If your child's Right Instrument is one for which there is not a great demand locally for tuition, it is unlikely there will be a full-time teacher. Partly for this reason, most professional musicians also teach. The national office of the Musicians' Union at 60/62 Clapham Road, London SW9 0JJ (Tel: 0207 840 5534), will give the address of the area office, from which you can obtain a list of members who play the instrument in question. The added glamour of learning from a player can be a source of motivation for the child.

Similarly, any mature music student should be equipped to teach children. It is quite normal to contact a music college, university or college music department and ask for the names of students who teach.

The First Lesson

A child's first music lesson is an important event. Dressing smartly or wearing a favourite item of clothing helps to foster this feeling.

The parent should bring a small notebook in which to write the teacher's instructions and details of the scales and pieces to be worked on at home during the week. Teachers are happy to answer questions about correct care of the instrument, which can avoid the damage many children inadvertently cause. Repairs to musical instruments are very expensive and best avoided.

Punctuality is important because music teachers structure their day tightly. Arriving early ensures that the child is not nervous about being late whereas rushing in at the last minute can ruin the first half of the lesson, especially on a wind instrument for which unstressed breathing is important. A nervous child may be calmed by a small snack while waiting.

Some teachers like the parent (but never siblings or friends!) to be present during the early lessons. Most private teachers give lessons in their own homes where there are no facilities for parents to wait.

Whereas a teacher at school is shared by twenty or thirty other children, the relationship between the music teacher and pupil is usually one-to-one. After the lesson some children want to chatter about this new experience and tell the parent about problems they encountered. Other children preserve what can be an unnerving silence about the whole event while they mull it over in their own minds. The parent must be ready to chatter or respect the child's desire for privacy according to temperament. There is only one taboo: the subject of music, which should be avoided, except by the parent who is a competent musician.

Parents may be disappointed if the lesson is shrugged off with some negative comment. If this happens, it is likely to be because the child has discovered in the first lesson that playing an instrument is not a game, but involves hard work. (It is confusing that the verb we use is *play*.) In such a case, the parent should gently point out that sportsmen, athletes, ice skaters, gymnasts, racing drivers all have to work if they are going to be good.

Perhaps the most fruitful way of rounding off the experience of the first lesson is for the child to play to other members of the family something that has been learnt at the lesson: a very simple tune or just a couple of notes on the fiddle is a modest achievement which deserves some applause.

Practising: Why is it Necessary?

Practice makes perfect! The old adage is never more true than in music. Playing an instrument is a process demanding a high degree of mental and physical co-ordination, far beyond what is necessary for any other childhood activity in or out of school.

Children accept that they must train regularly to acquire and improve sports technique, for example. They can understand that playing an instrument demands the same daily ritual. Parents can help by making a semantic parallel with other childhood activities and calling the daily instrumental exercises *training*. This is a modern word which has all the right connotations in the child's mind; by contrast *practice* sounds old-fashioned.

The parent who learnt an instrument in childhood needs no reminder of the importance of practice. However, the non-musical parent may not understand what is taking place during daily practice sessions. Neither parent nor child should regard them as a boring chore or meaningless repetition of a few set pieces, for it is regular practice that builds the co-ordination which eventually makes playing the instrument pleasurable and easy.

Repeating the same exercises day after day is also a way of transferring new learning from the current week's lesson out of the conscious mind into the subconscious. When the child can do a particular exercise 'without thinking about it' the conscious mind is free to accept the input of next week's lesson. The child who does not practice tends not to reach this stage. In his cluttered mind, unabsorbed knowledge becomes confused with the next lesson's input. This mental traffic jam produces confusion and can lead to a learning block which lasts a lifetime. *Even the best teacher's efforts are thrown away by the child who does not practice.*

Practising: How Long?

Ten minutes' practice each day is enough for most young children beginning an instrument. A longer period may produce boredom. The duration of practice builds naturally to twenty minutes and longer. A once-a-week session of half an hour crammed in just before the lesson is virtually useless and will not fool the teacher one little bit!

Initially, it is not important how long the child spends with the instrument. What is vital is to make practice an habitual part of the child's day like cleaning teeth or getting dressed. It is easier for the child if practice is always at the same time of day, e.g. early in the morning or before doing homework.

Some children like the parent to listen to what is being practised; some like to do it alone. A good teacher structures the practice schedule, usually by writing in the pupil's notebook the work to be done before the next lesson.

Positive Parenting Makes Practice Fun

Parents who can themselves play an instrument are able to 'sit in' on the daily practice sessions and encourage the young learner by accompanying him or her, playing simple duets together and demonstrating how the tunes should sound.

Happily, modern recording technology makes it easy for all parents to make practice fun by using books with demos and accompaniment on CDs. Play-along material ranges from beginner tutor books such as *Learn As You Play* and *Listen, Read and Play* and *Rock and Pop Scales*, which remove the boredom of practising the same scale again and again and again on one's own.

Apart from the self-contained instruments like keyboards and guitars, musical instruments were designed to play with others. Today, every child can have the satisfaction from very early on of playing with an electronic accompanist CD who never gets tired or bored even after a hundred repetitions!

Only the parent can personalize practice material. The teacher is following a basic course of instruction used for many different children, but the parent knows the particular child's tastes and enthusiasms. Whether for musicals or film themes, television tunes or classical music, somewhere on the shelves of any good music shop will be a corresponding choice of CD-based fun practice material. For computer-addicted children, there are also CD-Roms to play along with. These have the solo part on the screen or printed out and accompaniment from the computer speakers, which makes this system a hi-tech play-along chum, who also never gets bored!

Do not be discouraged if the child finds the written part difficult at first. Even just following the dots visually and listening, he or she is learning and eventually will be able to play along. The first results may sound awful to adult ears – whether rap, rock or Ravel – but to the junior star lost in the clouds of karaoke, the pleasure is only one step away from *Star Academy*.

Musical Literacy

Do children need to learn to read music? Musically illiterate jazz, folk and rock musicians are sometimes heard saying that learning to read music would kill their inspiration. How do they know?

As far as a child is concerned, there is no point in learning an instrument and failing to become musically literate, for this leaves the young musician – however good at his instrument – in a limbo where each piece of music has to be memorized or improvised, where it is difficult to play with others and where one's choice of music to play is severely limited.

Compare this situation with that of the child who comes to read music as a natural part of learning the instrument. Without any extra effort, he will have the immense repertoire of all the great composers open to him. He can choose to play whatever kind of music suits his temperament. He can sit down in a band or orchestra and play music he has never seen before.

To become a fully fledged musician, it is vital to learn to read music. Learning an instrument without the ability to read music can be likened to living in a library without the key that opens the bookcase.

'Musical Dyslexia'

Music written for the self-contained instruments, especially piano, is far more complicated to decipher than music for single-note instruments. Most children who develop 'musical dyslexia' do so as a result of trying to unscramble chords (groups of notes played simultaneously) and music written in two clefs for the piano. Once implanted, such a mental block lasts usually for life.

This is not a reflection of how intelligent the child is, or how musical; thousands of very bright children find it impossible mentally to process several notes at the same time.

At the first sign that this is happening to your child, discuss the problem with a teacher. Do not accept any advice which implies that your child is unmusical or in any way at fault. If the problem continues and the child begins to cheat by memorizing each piece and never actually reading a note of the written music, try the simplest of all remedies: use the Ben-Tovim/Boyd System to find the most suitable single-note instrument. The music for these instruments is so easy to read by comparison with keyboard music that most children transferring to them soar ahead with sheer relief at being released from the terrors of piano notation! There are few children who find problems in reading music for woodwind, brass or strings.

Who Needs Theory?

A knowledge of theory or 'the rudiments of music' is an intrinsic part of a comprehensive musical education.

A conscientious teacher weaves a strand of musical theory throughout the course of instrumental tuition. If presented in the form of simple tests and quizzes where each question has only one correct answer – like a classroom test at school – most children absorb basic theory quite easily. Pianists who are familiar with chords and the bass clef take to theory like ducks to water.

The only identifiable group of children who find theory difficult are those whose teachers have ignored it completely until after Grade 5 of the Associated Board examination syllabus. In order to take further instrumental examinations, the child may have to pass the Grade 5 theory paper. The written questions are not in themselves difficult for a student at this stage of musical development, but if theory has previously been neglected by the teacher, the child is tempted to regard it as a boring chore, unrelated to the business of learning an instrument.

148

Aural Training

Aural tests form part of all music examinations: singing a note played on the piano, clapping a rhythm, recognizing intervals, beating time, etc. Such tests measure aural perception. Some children have a naturally acute ear and find the tests easy; others need more training. Any child who sings in a choir finds aural training easy.

Arguably, woodwind-players only need aural training in order to play with others. At the other extreme, string-players need a high level of aural acuity from the first stages of learning, while brass-players without a sense of pitch couldn't find the first note of a tune.

Should Children Take Music Exams?

A small number of parents believe that any competition or examination is bad for their child's psychological development. However, almost all children are so used to tests and exams at school that only an exceptionally fragile child is traumatized by taking a music exam. In any case, few children risk the humiliation of failure in these examinations because music teachers only enter children who are ready to take a particular grade.

The examinations cover all the stages of learning an instrument from the very first steps to a professional diploma. They are not competitive, so nobody is top or bottom but children who are talented or have worked hard can gain Merit or Distinction certificates.

The instrumental examinations are not written tests. They are formal but relaxed performances of set pieces on which the child has worked with the teacher for months, combined with a short aural test, one or two scales and some appropriate sight reading.

Working for an examination gives the child an incentive. Receiving the certificate provides a sense of achievement; it is a recognition by an important body that the child has done a good job and is one step further along the path to making music.

The examination system serves an additional purpose for the non-musical parent who finds it impossible to judge whether a particular teacher is good or bad, except by hearsay. Any teacher who enters his pupils for examinations set by the Associated Board of the Royal Schools of Music, or one of the other recognized bodies, must follow a carefully structured curriculum. Indirectly, therefore, the exams give the parent a guarantee that the child is receiving a balanced course of musical education.

Passing the graded examinations at regular intervals is the best evidence for a parent that progress is being satisfactorily maintained. Parents should not under-estimate the achievement of passing even the lower grades. At every level, the successful candidate deserves sincere congratulations.

Playing in Public: Coping with Nerves

Some children are nervous at the idea of having to play in front of a stranger. The examiners understand this. Speaking on behalf of his colleagues, one of them admitted to the authors that he would be equally shy if he had to play in front of the children and their parents!

A few tips:

- arrange for the child to play the set pieces as often as possible in the week before the exam to anyone who can be persuaded to be a mock examiner;
- a proper meal before going to the exam centre gives energy when needed;

- a new item of comfortable clothing can give a little extra confidence;
- before leaving home, check that the child has the right music to play;
- arrive early to avoid panic. (If the examination centre is in a congested part of a town, do a trial run beforehand to check parking problems, etc.);
- a drink of water while waiting is a good idea (but wind players should avoid any sweet drink or fruit);
- bring spare reeds, strings or whatever – just in case;
- no lipstick for the girl playing a wind instrument!

Generally speaking, the younger a child begins to take exams and play in public, the less likely he is to develop 'nerves'. On the contrary, the child who has taken a series of music exams over the years of learning acquires a self-confidence in public that other children lack and which will stand him or her in good stead later in life at job interviews or on other occasions when a 'performance' is required.

What to Do when Interest Flags

Probably all children play psychological games with their parents sometimes. Skipping the daily practice session or cutting it progressively shorter may be a game. It could alternatively be a sign that the child has genuinely lost interest in music. Even the happiest child, matched with the right instrument and learning from a good teacher can sometimes lose impetus.

What can a parent do to help?

With younger children, a present like a music stand, a new music case or even something as small as a musical badge or notebook can bring the fun back into music. Sitting down with the child to watch a music programme on television costs nothing and can mean a lot. A visit to a live concert or other event where the instrument being learnt can be seen in action may be the exciting stimulus needed to break the negative syndrome. Older children may respond similarly to a new record or cassette of a musical hero or heroine.

Children whose musical activity is restricted to the weekly lesson and daily practice on their own at home may simply be *bored*! If that sounds strange, bear in mind that the point of learning an instrument is to make music, not to sit alone practising scales and arpeggios. While the piano, harp or guitar can make complete music on their own, endlessly playing little tunes on flute or cornet by oneself is not terribly exciting for a sociable child. All the single-note instruments need to be played with others in order to produce harmony. Once a child can read music and makes a good quality of sound, the parent can obviate boredom by finding opportunities for the child to play with others and make 'real music'.

The Social Side of Music

Welding a number of children of varying abilities into a musical ensemble is a job for a skilled professional. Simply assembling several children who learn instruments and hoping they can have a musical party is unrealistic. The level of instrumental skill, musical literacy and musicianship required to play with others is higher than a non-musician thinks.

Yet with the exception of the self-contained instruments, the greatest joy of playing comes from making music in bands, orchestras, chamber groups or other ensembles.

With the exception of brass bands, which are autonomous and run their own junior sections, most music groups which a child can join are run by the school system. Some private schools of music have their own ensembles which give end-of-term performances. Most large secondary schools have their own junior and senior orchestras. The school music teacher should be able to recommend where the young musician can play. In some areas there are music centres in or out of school hours which provide facilities and coaching for less formal music-making activities such as dance bands, wind bands, concert bands, recorder groups – even pop groups.

Becoming a regular member of an orchestra, band or group is a wonderful opportunity for any musical child to find like-minded friends. The younger children derive great satisfaction and stimulus from mixing freely with the older players – a social phenomenon which is unique to music. No nine-year-old can play football or netball against eighteen-year-olds, but he can play music with them!

Changing Teachers

Sometimes a child who has been learning for several years, has passed exams and perhaps plays in a band or orchestra, will suddenly 'go off' practising, resent going to lessons and generally become difficult about music. Why?

Many children need to change teachers once or twice during their years of learning. This does not mean that the former teacher is bad, but simply that the relationship which worked well for an eight-year-old is unsuitable for the same child five years later. A change of teacher may cause an adolescent to take a fresh interest in music.

Music teachers are quite used to losing pupils in this way; there is no need for a parent to feel embarrassed, so long as any agreed period of notice is adhered to.

Learning a Second Instrument

The process of instrumental learning extends through the years of adolescence when the child's personality is undergoing much change. A teenager may reject music precisely because it is an activity known to have strong parental approval. It is also possible that the adolescent has a quite reasonable feeling that 'I was not consulted about the choice of instrument I had to learn', which makes music a good field for rebellion.

Some parents fight their adolescent offspring, while others concede increasing independence. In the latter case, the best help a parent can give is to use the Ben-Tovim/Boyd System to find a second instrument. All that was learnt on the first instrument will come in useful, for nothing is wasted in music. Learning a second instrument is like learning a second foreign language belonging to the same linguistic group: it's a thousand times easier than the first.

The sudden take-off on the second instrument can lift the teenager's mental sights to new musical horizons.

When choosing a second instrument, it is worthwhile to consider the 'endangered species'. Not bison, but bassoons and basses. Not tigers, but tubas. Every youth orchestra is short of players for the bass instruments, because they are rarely the first choice and are inappropriate for small bodies. But the adolescent who is growing bored with a higher-register first instrument gets great satisfaction on these large instruments. Progress is very rapid because the parts are not difficult to read. Few parents mind the chore of transportation for an adolescent whose new instrument is a passport to the positive cultural and social environment of youth orchestras, ensembles and concert bands.

There is also a very worthwhile hidden bonus! Mention

of competence on two instruments, especially if one is an 'endangered species', on an UCAS application form can make the difference between the university or course of first choice and having to take second best.

Assessing the Talent of the Child

How can a parent – even one who learnt an instrument in childhood – accurately assess a child's musical talent?

In general, the teacher's comments and the completely objective examination results are the best indicators of how talented a child is. There are also several systems which supposedly test the musical ability of children. Such tests are administered by trained teachers. In practice, they measure aural sensitivity to pitch and rhythm and the sense of harmony. They do not measure musical ability.

Conductors of junior orchestras are constantly on the lookout for talent. If your child has talent, almost certainly a teacher will tell you. Yet it is possible for a child to slip through the net. If you believe that your child is especially talented but nobody else shares your opinion, what can you do?

It goes without saying that such a child has gained high marks in several exams (high Distinctions), performs consistently well and without nerves in public, enjoys practising and obviously derives great pleasure from making and listening to music.

The simplest course for the parent is to approach the relevant principal of the nearest symphony orchestra or contact the nearest music college or university music department and ask to pay for an assessment lesson. In thirty or sixty minutes, you will be left in no doubt as to how your child compares with the general run of children learning the same instrument. The assessor will also give expert advice on the instrument ('is it good enough?') and the teacher ('is he/she good enough for this child?').

Prodigies

Prodigies occur in three fields: chess, mathematics and music. Most musical prodigies are produced by musical families. Essentially, a musical prodigy is a child who learns to play one or more instruments so quickly that he or she seems to have little need of a teacher; it is obvious to both parent and teacher almost from the first time the child picks up the instrument that another Menuhin or Mozart has been born.

Does that sound a wonderful thing for the parents? Beware! One of the dictionary definitions of the word prodigy is: *a monster*. A prodigy can indeed be a monster who takes over the whole family. He or she devotes the greater part of each day to music; schoolwork comes a poor second priority.

Parents never have to bully or cajole this child into practising; the problem is to stop the practising for meals or to get the child to bed at a reasonable hour. One weekly lesson is insufficient because the prodigy moves too fast. Two or three lessons from an excellent teacher may not suffice, in which case the prodigy has to make monthly accompanied trips to London or another major city for supplementary lessons. He or she may play in several orchestras, requiring transport to and from several different towns each week. Usually one parent becomes in effect the prodigy's full-time manager, while the other members of the family become second-class citizens.

Not every prodigy becomes an outstanding or even a run-of-the-mill professional musician. Some rebel at adolescence and never play another note, some develop repeated stress syndrome from playing too much too young, some have nervous breakdowns and some . . . just run out of steam. Almost all ex-prodigies suffer from their abnormal childhood.

Specialist Music Schools

A considerable number of children are talented but below the level which could be called prodigious. Specialist music schools are designed to take these children and from them produce the cream of the nation's professional musicians. A few prodigies are also to be found there.

Such schools combine a general educational curriculum with an intense and uncompromising musical education. Entrance is highly competitive from age eight upwards. A pupil's day may start at six a.m. with supervised practice and continue until late in the evening with little or no spare time. Some children who want only to make music find this life sheer bliss; others crack up or conceal their private misery for years, not wanting to let their parents and teachers down.

At these schools the standard of musical tuition and the facilities for developing instrumental ability and musicianship are of the best. Compulsory lessons include theory, harmony, aural training, choir, orchestra, music history and composition as well as instrumental tuition on two or three instruments.

There is never any shortage of like-minded friends for the child whose only interest is music. Some schools are boarding-only; others accept day pupils. In either case, the school takes over from the parent total responsibility for the child's educational and musical development. In certain cases, the school also assumes financial responsibility, even to the extent of providing professional-quality instruments for the children.

If there is one criticism of these schools which a parent needs to bear in mind, it is that they inevitably narrow a child's outlook. Former pupils who do not succeed in a musical career tend to regard themselves as failures.

To find out more about the specialist schools, a parent whose child can demonstrate outstanding musical ability should contact the local education authority for advice. Alternatively, the public library should have *Music Education Yearbook* available for reference. This publication lists all the specialist music schools.

Competitions: are they Good or Bad?

In addition to the highly publicized media events like the BBC's *Young Musician of the Year*, there are many music festivals, school and music-centre competitions, as well as competitions for young musicians run by public and private organizations.

At a local level, entering a competitive festival need not be stressful. It is a chance to perform in a friendly but serious atmosphere. A child who enjoys competing with others and playing in public, finds it fun to be pitted against children of roughly similar standard. Competing is also a healthy way of finding out the answer to the question: 'How good am I, compared with other children of my age/length of learning?'

Children nervous before playing in competitions or concerts can be helped by the same tips that work so well before an exam.

Parents who are unsure how to assess their own child's talent can learn a lot by simply listening to the other competitors and comparing.

The judges' remarks are always helpful and encouraging. Many judges make themselves accessible during the intervals for advice about tuition, instruments, technique or trying for a specialist music school.

Brass-band competitions and competitions for youth orchestras do not put the individual performer on trial. They are exciting social events which weld the ensemble together.

The high-powered media competitions are different. They are run as gladiatorial eliminations to fascinate and excite mass audiences. This is a fair game for young professionals but a risky business for children and students to get involved in. Such events may make exciting viewing for those watching at home but they risk over-inflating the ego of the winners and seriously demoralizing less mature players. Either way, taking part in these competitions has distorted many a young player's career.

Children with Special Physical Needs

Many children with physical difficulties do learn to play instruments for their own pleasure and satisfaction. For most of them, music-making is one activity in which they can compete on equal terms with their peer group, even if special transportation and seating arrangements have to be made for them.

Since children with physical difficulties have encountered so many 'things I cannot do like other children', it is crucial that adults involved in the selection of instruments concentrate realistically on the aspect of physical suitability. The golden rule is that the instruments must suit the child, not the other way round. If nine out of ten children fail to learn a badly selected instrument, the odds against a bad choice succeeding for a child who has physical difficulties are immense. When in doubt, change the instrument rather than demoralize the child.

Except in the most severe cases, it is always possible to find some instrument on which a child with special physical needs can produce a sound. Modern electronic instruments, for example, require almost no physical effort. If the instrument has to be held in an unorthodox position or with the help of some strap or brace, never mind. Children with physical difficulties are used to working out different ways of doing things for themselves.

The mouth is one of the most sensitive and versatile parts of the human body. Thus brass instruments, on which most of the work of making sound is done by the muscles of the lips and diaphragm, are particularly worth consideration where limbs are lacking or dysfunctional. An additional factor in the choice of this family of instruments is that brass-players are relaxed and friendly (except when locked in life-and-death competitions!). In the sociable atmosphere of a junior brass band a child with physical difficulties can be accepted on his or her musical merits.

Children with Special Learning Difficulties

Music therapy is a field of work which has been transformed in the two decades since the first edition of this book. There are now in Britain many thousands of specially trained music therapists and many useful books on the subject readily available.

Percussion instruments and the brass – which gives most physical feed-back to the player and are technically robust – are generally favoured in preference to stringed instruments, which are simple of construction but very hard to play and fragile, and the woodwind family, which have so many moving parts to manipulate and can easily be damaged.

There is little place in a book like this for personal anecdote. Yet the authors remember with emotion an incident which took place after Atarah's Band had played at the Perth Festival in Scotland. We received an invitation to visit a home for children with Down's syndrome. Some of the children had been brought to the concert, but most were unable to travel, hence the invitation. An impromptu musical party was given for them by the musicians. At the end of the party the children sang a thank-you song.

We did not know until afterwards that most of the children singing could not speak. Yet, due to the devotion of an exceptional teacher, they were able to sing. No educationist can measure such an achievement, but it was a small musical miracle.

Learning an Instrument as Emotional Therapy

Any parent whose child has emotional problems such as hyperactivity, excessive introversion, outbursts of temper or shyness with other children will spend a good deal of thought on the emotional requirements and rewards of the different instruments. For any child, from the complete introvert to the physically violent, there is a choice of instruments, the learning of which will be positive therapy. An in-built benefit of learning is the developing one-to-one relationship with the teacher.

Some children who dislike most social groups find that they are able to take part in bands or orchestras with enjoyment, perhaps because they are too busy thinking about their instrument and the written music in front of them to be aware of themselves.

Becoming a Professional Musician

Most parents are impressed when their child learns to play the first tune on an instrument. Where will it lead?

Fleetingly perhaps, the parent wonders if this is the first step on the path to becoming a professional musician.

It's possible, but the facts are not encouraging. Per head of population, there are fewer jobs for musicians today than before the age of canned music. Professional musicians have to compete for their daily bread. For an advertised orchestral vacancy there can be as many as two hundred applicants all technically good enough to do the job – and all of them far better players than the local music teacher.

With few exceptions, musicians do not enjoy the luxury of paid holidays, pension schemes, sick pay and the other securities of modern life which most people take for granted. They live in a world of a harsh Victorian reality where one must be outstandingly good to survive. Most musicians in Britain are freelance: they sit at home waiting for the telephone to ring. The music business is a very risky profession. Even those who are good enough to get work and survive, know that they have no long-term guarantee of prosperity; if their standard of playing falls off for any reason, the telephone stops ringing.

The pop world is even more chancy: for every group that makes it in the charts, there are thousands of others who don't. Some successful rock and pop artistes have had a conventional musical education; some are musically illiterate millionaires.

Other Careers with Music

Parents sometimes ask whether the time spent learning an instrument is wasted 'when it could be devoted to homework, maybe resulting in one more pass at GCSE.' In addition to a career as a professional musician, there are many hundreds of jobs where the knowledge of music which results from learning to play an instrument is an essential requirement. For thousands more jobs, a pass at Grade 6 or 8 – or having gone on tour with the County Youth Orchestra – may be the bonus point which helps your child to beat the other applicants. Among careers which music can open to your child are:

junior and secondary school class teaching; private teaching; instrumental teaching within the school system; arts administration; sound engineering; a thousand different jobs in television, radio and recording studios; composing and arranging; film editing; production of commercials; publishing; lecturing; acoustic research; electronics; making and repairing instruments; choral training; conducting; selling music and instruments; concert agency and management; pop promotions; Leisure Service jobs in local authorities; music therapy; librarianship; computer programming; disc jockeying; all the performing arts and many others.

In a job-scarce world, the ability to play an instrument may be more than just a leisure activity for your child.